LIKE
FINDING
Water in
THE DESERT

THE INSPIRING STORIES OF FOUR WOMEN

Betty Viamontes • Anna Brubaker
Susana Jiménez-Mueller • Jean Morciglio, Ph.D.

DEDICATION

This anthology is dedicated to our families and to people who may be struggling to find the inspiration for a new beginning.

FOREWORD

The idea for this anthology originated from the friendship of Jean Morciglio, Susana Jiménez-Mueller, and Anna Brubaker, participants in the Life Story Writing program and the Bloomingdale Writers Connection writing circles, at the Bloomingdale Regional Library, in Valrico, FL.

Betty Viamontes, a local Hillsborough County leader, joined them in writing and compiling their stories; all are hoping to inspire our youth and influence the way America sees Hispanic women.

As my teacher and mentor for the writing program, the late Dr. James E. Birren, once wrote.

"As each generation moves into adulthood, the past assumes greater significance. Our accumulated life experiences often take us on an unexpected journey in search of answers. We start compiling our family history. In this age of instant technology, looking backwards can be a giant step forward. Clarity emerges from reflection. We live our lives in the moment, but each step resonates with the learning we have brought with us. The wisdom we gain is a gift that we can share with those who come after us. We can now pass down our life stories to family, friends, and institutions."

The authors of this book realized the possibilities and accepted the opportunity. Enjoy!

Val Perry
Coordinator of the Bloomingdale Writers Connection (BWC) and an Instructor/Coordinator of the Bloomingdale Life Story Writing classes.
BWC offers classes to assist people in writing their life stories at Bloomingdale Regional Library, sponsors life-writing events, and helps organize monthly life writing groups to support the writers in meeting their writing goals.
Lifewritersbloom@msn.com.

CONTENTS

ACKNOWLEDGMENTS

The co-authors would like to thank Arielle Haughee, the Bloomingdale Writers Connection, Mike Birch, Rose Ann Froberg, Bryce Moseley Photography, Rebeca Mueller, Val Perry, Lissette Riley, Kayrene Smither, Keren Vergon, and Ivan Viamontes for supporting the *Like Finding Water in the Desert* anthology project. A special thanks to our readers for their unparalleled patronage.

RECLAIMING

Betty Viamontes

PROLOGUE

I'm standing in front of a crowd of almost five-hundred people. I begin my speech, but I can hardly see past the stage because the lights blind me. Yet, I know that somewhere among the spectators is my family. Some have come from Miami and Orlando. Others live here in Tampa, but the person who made it all possible is not among them.

I'm fifty-four years old, and a long journey of love and loss has brought me here. I'm Tampa's Hispanic Heritage Inc. Woman of the Year. Local television channels, radio personalities, and newspaper columnists have interviewed me, which has allowed me to record my story permanently in the history of Tampa, Florida, the city I'm proud to call home.

If I could only see her for a few minutes and show her that since she left, I have worked harder than ever before to make her proud and share her story. She didn't want the world to forget what happened to her and to others like her, and I won't stop until I see her life on the big screen.

Many said I was wasting my time publishing her story. "No one will read it," they said. But readers embraced it, even a women's book club from the United Nations. It took me fourteen years to write it, and after it was done, the marketing, public appearances, and book signings began. I have received notes and letters from so many people inspired by her life that I knew I had to keep writing. Five books so far, not including this collaboration written by women just like me, lost for so long.

Yet, somehow, each of us kept searching in the desert that had become our lives for that sip of water that would help us keep moving. One foot in front of the other. That is what it took. We looked back only to propel us forward. No regrets. Our past was the prize we had to pay to become who we are.

ALONE

After leaving the school Zambrana in Havana's Santos Suárez neighborhood, Clarisa takes my handful of textbooks, places them on top of hers, and we walk home. She lives a block away from me in a three-story apartment building on Zapote Street, and since the first day we met, she has been carrying my books. A third grader and much taller than me, she has braided hair and a runner's legs. I'm only a first grader and not strong enough to hold such a heavy load. It makes my arms sore.

When my mother found out I allowed someone else to do what I should be doing, she wasn't happy. My five-year-old sister's statement, "Mami, Betty thinks she's a princess. She's always making people do stuff for her," only added fuel to the fire.

"That's not true!" I said. "I was hot and tired. I gave her my books and said 'here, take these.' She's very nice, so she did. Since then, she carries them for me. What's wrong with that?"

"You should carry your own books. Life will not always be easy, you know." Mamá replied.

I didn't understand why Mamá made such a big deal about it. I crossed my arms, stamped my feet, and glared at her and my younger sister.

The next day, when Clarisa offers to carry them, my mother's words echo in my head: *You should carry your own books.* I hesitate for a moment.

"Thank you. I think I'll carry them myself," I say with a hint of self-pity.

Clarisa doesn't insist. She walks by my side and watches how I switch them from one arm to the other, or hold them with both arms, hoping to even out the weight. She smiles and says nothing.

The sun cooks the broken concrete. My school uniform's white blouse sticks to my back as we pass by the old colonial-style houses in various stages of disrepair. I'm drenched in sweat, unsure if I will make it home without fainting. Not even the flamboyant trees in their orange dresses can protect me from the heat. My legs tremble. If I had eaten my lunch, maybe I wouldn't feel this way. I'm just not in the mood to eat very much. It's been that way since my father left for the United States three years ago.

My mother tries force-feeding me. That doesn't work. I look at her with disgust and spit out the food. To add to my frustration, for the last two weeks she's been serving me split-pea soup for lunch and dinner.

"There isn't much variety at the stores. Eat your food," she says.

"I'm tired of eating *chícharos,* Mamá! I'm starting to see them in my dreams."

She tells me that's what she can buy with her government-issued ration card, so we have no choice other than to buy food on the black market at exorbitant prices.

"Why don't you go to Elio's house in Güira? He has vegetables you can use to make *ajiaco*. I like ajiaco."

That is one of my favorite foods. Mamá makes it for my brother— a mixture of all the vegetables she brings from Elio's farm and any meat she can find. My sister and I can only have a little because it's too expensive to make, and my brother needs it.

"Your grandpa has been sick! You know that."

I shrug my shoulders.

Elio, a farmer who lives in Güira de Melena with his wife, sells fruits and vegetables he cultivates on his farm to Mamá. Sometimes, instead of money, she gives him soap she brings from Havana. Mamá tells me that every time she goes to Güira and brings back more than the twenty-five pounds allowed by the government, she risks going to jail or having the goods confiscated by the authorities. She always exceeds the limit. To avoid attracting attention from the police, she spreads the weight among us. She has no choice. It takes over two hours to get to Havana's countryside by bus, not to mention the walk to Elio's house accompanied by her three small children. My brother, who has severe food allergies, gets tired sometimes, and she must carry him in her arms. Other times it's so hot that we stop for a glass of water at one of the town's tiny houses along the way.

I love to visit Elio because he and his wife give me the sweetest chunks of mamey fruit I have ever eaten. After I finish my fruit, I look at them, as if waiting for a second serving. "You want another piece?" Elio asks. I know Mamá doesn't let me ask for seconds, so I look down, knowing the second piece will soon follow. I can't wait until my *abuelo*, grandfather, gets better, so we can return to the country. He and Mamá have been very sad since my maternal grandmother died.

Sometimes, on weekends, I ask Mamá to buy me pizza from the Sorrento Pizzeria near our house. For one peso and twenty cents, we can buy a personal pie I would love to eat by myself. However, I'm not allowed. Mamá only makes one-hundred pesos a month at the bodega and insists I share with my youngest sister Lissette, while Mamá shares hers with my little brother Rene. Too bad we can only afford to buy it once a month.

So, I eat when I feel like it, which has made me frail and landed me at the hospital twice with pneumonia since my father left three years ago. I was three years old then. He went to the United States, a magical place, from what Mamá tells me. Mamá thought we would be able to leave Cuba to join him, but she received a letter recently that made her cry more than usual. She says she doesn't know how long it will be before we see Papá again.

Clarisa and I are almost at the corner of Serrano and Zapote. A little longer and I'll be home. I want to tell my mother that this time I carried my own books and achieved another 100 on my Math test. That will please her. She needs some happiness. I don't like to see her so sad when she gets home from work.

I say goodbye to Clarisa and climb the five tiled steps leading to the front porch of the colonial-style house where I live. I push the unlocked door and start calling Mamá's name. I don't know if she's home because she works so many hours, but sometimes she assigns work to her students in the classroom down the street and leaves to prepare food for us. The house seems eerily quiet. I walk past the living room into the tiny dining room. It's hot inside and all the windows are closed. I call her name again. No answer.

I smell something in the air. Not sure what it is. Then I hear someone crying.

"Mamá?"

Her crying leads me to her. I just know I will make her happy when I tell her the news. That will dry her tears, so I rush to her bedroom.

When I enter, our glances meet. My smile fades in an instant. I'm trying to process what I'm seeing, but nothing makes sense. The smell is much stronger now. I recognize it. It's what Mamá uses to refill the Chinese lamps when the electricity goes out. Her hair and clothes are soaked, and I see an empty bottle on the bed. With the boxes of matches in her hand, she weeps and tells me she's sorry. I don't have time to ask why. All I know is that if I wait one more minute, it will be too late.

I run to her and take the matches from her hand without saying a word. Tears cloud my vision, and as much as I despise running, I have to give it my all.

I sprint out to the street and climb the stairs of the colonial house next door. As I do, I think about my aunt and uncle, but they're at work, and my brother and sister went to the doctor with my grandparents. I have no choice but to ask the neighbors for help.

Zapote Street is quiet. I scream, "*¡Por favor ayude a mi mamá!* Please help my mother!" and knock as hard as I can, many times, until someone opens. By then, other neighbors have come out of their houses to see what's going on.

I race back home, and several neighbors follow. I try to go inside the house, but a woman grabs my hand and insists I stay outside. I tremble, and tears roll down my face.

As I pace around the porch, playing with my clammy hands, I remember Mamá's words again: *You should carry your own books.*

I look down. I understand what she means now…

Sorrow fills me.

Papá left us, and I'm afraid to lose Mamá, but I will never tell her how I feel because I don't want to see her sad.

I won't tell anyone what I saw. I must carry my pain like I carried my books today.

Alone.

SWEET FIFTEEN

1980

I stand in front of the mirror on this cool February evening while Mamá powders my face.

"Mamá, I need to go outside. People are waiting!"

"Betty, stop rushing me. I want the pictures I send to your father to be perfect."

Betty, that's what she calls me, but my given name is Beatriz, a name that my paternal grandmother tells me means Bringer of Joy. On this day, I don't think I'm bringing joy to anyone, especially to Mamá.

"I'm tired of staying in this room!" I say waving my manicured hands.

She ignores me and straightens my dress.

I don't look like myself. Makeup covers the redness left after seven acne-removal treatments at the beauty salon. My skin looks flawless. A thin black line beneath my hazel eyes brings them to life, and for the first time, I feel pretty. I fear this feeling will be temporary, like in Cinderella.

Mamá took me to one of the best beauty parlors in Havana. I asked her why she didn't get her hair done at the salon, but she said it was too much money, so she put her hair up in rollers when we returned home.

The house, packed with teenagers awaiting my entrance into the courtyard, radiates with joy, dancing, and laughter in celebration of my *Quince Años*. I can't believe I'm fifteen. My birthday was on Friday, but the party is today. Not much has changed since my father left eleven years and four months ago. Every month, Mamá reminds me how long it has been, like a monthiversary. He's still in the United States, and we in Cuba, the Caribbean island that keeps deteriorating like an old shoe, but I don't care. I'm moving on. Happy at last, I glow like a Chinese lamp on a blackout night.

In preparation for the party, Mamá pays attention to every detail: the swans that decorate my cake, the photographer who documents this event, even the house where my celebration is held. Our home, with its cracking ceilings supported by wooden trusses, lacks the conditions for a party. However, Amparo, the lady who teaches Spanish dances in the neighborhood, *she* has an amazing house.

It looks like a museum.

Built in the late 1800s, it is the picture of perfection—from the elaborate tile floors, to the gold and red bedspreads that a relative sent her from the United States, to the bouquets of real flowers in several rooms. She probably has wealthy relatives who send her money to keep her house looking like this. Amparo must have felt sorry for Mamá, after watching her raise three children on her own for so many years. Only that would explain her generosity.

Mamá doesn't let me leave the bedroom until she makes sure I don't have a hair out of place. By the time I walk out into the courtyard wearing a long muslin dress, all eyes turn to me with looks of amazement. Then, the music changes to a slow song by the Bee Gees. I dance with a boy I met just a couple of days ago. His father belongs to the Communist Party, and he's the only one in the neighborhood who owns a suit. That's what Mamá told me.

While we dance, my boyfriend glances at me from the crowd. I whisper, "I'm sorry." The cool February breeze plays with my hair, and I smell the aroma of jasmine. I recognize it because my boyfriend picked up a few for me the night before. I wish I could dance with him, but Mamá says he's not dressed for the occasion. As I dance, surrounded by six swirling couples, my long brown curls bounce. Later, my sister tells me I looked like an aristocrat from Cuba's bygone years.

After a while, the music stops, and a song that's popular in Miami circles for this type of celebration, *De Niña a Mujer,* begins to play. It is meant to be danced with one's father and highlights the sense of loss fathers feel when their daughter becomes a woman.

My uncle, the only father I've known for ten years, dances with me. His hands are cold and clammy, and he wipes a tear. I don't know why. He came to live at Mamá's house when I was about five after he and

11

my aunt got married. He and my aunt always buy me presents, help me with my homework, and take me out for pizza. I taught him how to dance, but he's not very good. He's a bit of a nerd, with big eyeglasses and a constant need to read. He enjoys engineering books mainly and listens to the prohibited radio station, *La Voz de las Américas*, in a room without windows. I join him sometimes. I can't tell anyone outside the house that he listens to that station. He can get in trouble. This radio station is his window to the outside world, to a place where the government doesn't control the media, and people can say what they think, or listen to foreign stations without fear.

My uncle loves reading so much he almost got run over by a car when he was crossing the street the other day. It has happened twice in recent years.

Mamá doesn't relax throughout the evening. She coordinates the pictures the photographer takes as if she has a mental list: one with the owners of the house, another with my grandmother, a third with my siblings and her. I lose count of how many more pictures the photographer snaps while the crowd gathers near us. This will cost her a fortune.

After a while, she doesn't let any more kids come into the courtyard. "The house is too full, and we're going to run out of food," she says, noticing people she didn't invite had come.

She makes me change several times with dresses my father sent from the United States, dresses no one in my neighborhood can afford. I feel special.

This night has taken years to orchestrate. Only someone like Mamá could have pulled it off. People say that necessity is the mother of invention, and Mamá is a master at "inventing."

In a country where having a business is illegal, she buys eye pencils on the black market for one peso and sells them for twenty pesos. People think my father sends them to her from the United States, so they don't mind paying premium prices for them. She doesn't tell people the truth. She says they're entitled to their own conclusions. For eight hours a day, she walks to multiple bodegas to pick up the money they collected and take it to a central business office. Each weekday, she also works as a teacher for four hours. Watching her work so much makes me admire her. Other than not being able to get us out of Cuba, it seems there's nothing she can't do.

By now, I believe she has given up on her dream to reunite with my father in the United States. She hasn't told me so, but she doesn't cry as much as she used to.

After my birthday, life at home goes back to normal, although it's becoming evident the conditions in Cuba are making people feel restless. That's what Mamá tells me. She says more of her friends are talking about leaving. A couple of people she knew killed themselves in the past year. She said they lost hope. One jumped off an apartment building in our Santos Suarez neighborhood, and another set herself on fire. This brings back bad memories I tried to forget. Easier said than done. A recurring nightmare haunts me. I'm inside a three-dimensional box, like those we draw in my geometry class. The box keeps shrinking, and just when it's about to crush me like a bug, I wake up sweating. I've never told anyone, not even my boyfriend.

One Sunday afternoon, in the middle of March, people's discontent takes form right in front of us when we're returning from the beach. I had never seen Fidel Castro in person until that day. Our bus suddenly stops, and people start yelling: "It's Fidel! He's behind us in a Jeep!" We all rush to the back of the bus to take a look.

It's him!

I see the man who has made my mother cry so much all these years. He hides behind a foggy glass, and when I distinguish his bearded face, my fists close in anger. Armed guards surround his Jeep. People are gathered on the streets protesting the lack of freedom and meager food rations with chants and signs. Until that day, no one dared to speak up. This is the start of something big. Even inside our bus, people argue with each other; and the pent-up fear to speak up suffers a blow in front of my eyes.

Two weeks later, on April 1, 1980, an event takes place that changes everything.

Tired of empty promises of improvements that never come, a group of men and women drive a bus through the gates of the Peruvian Embassy in Havana to ask for political asylum. Fidel Castro asks embassy officials to turn the offenders over to the authorities. They refuse. In retribution, he removes the guards from the entrance. Overnight, thousands of people of all ages inundate the embassy, provoking an unprecedented humanitarian crisis when the food and water run out.

My neighborhood is in turmoil. People rush to my house and tell Mamá, "If you go to the embassy, I will too." She's worried about her children and decides to stay home.

As the days pass, rumors take a new dimension when people start to disappear from the neighborhood. Everyone knows where they are.

After a while, Castro realizes he needs the internal pressure within the island to escape, or he will lose control of the country, as people from every province continue to travel to Havana to get into the embassy.

One evening, he makes an unexpected announcement on television. *All of those people in the United States with relatives in Cuba who want to come pick them up by boat at the Port of Mariel can do so.* Shocked, Mamá asks Tía Berta if she had heard right. My aunt nods. Mamá doesn't waste any time. She rushes out of the house and doesn't tell us where she's going.

Two nights later, I'm on the porch saying goodnight to my boyfriend and we kiss, without realizing my mother is watching us through the window.

I would never see him again.

Around two o'clock that evening, loud knocks awake us. When my mother opens the door, still sleepy from a long workday, armed guards rush in and order us to get dressed and not take anything. They tell us my father is waiting at the Port of Mariel.

"What's going on, Mamá?" I ask her.

"Just get dressed."

"But… you never said anything."

She ignores me and orders me to hurry. Moments later, one of the officials begins to read the names of the people who should accompany him. I hear "Lissette" (my sister), "Rene" (my brother), "Milagros" (my mom), "Justa Pastora" (my grandmother), and "Beatriz" (me). My aunt and uncle are not on the list. Mamá doesn't know why because my father claimed them and their daughters. Mamá argues with the officer, but Tia Berta, who has been awakened by the yelling, asks my mother to leave with us and not to worry about her and her family.

"It's your turn to be happy," she tells her. "We'll be okay."

I leave everything behind: my writing journals—those that saved me after my mother attempted to end her life—my Spanish language, my childhood friends, and the two people who had been my parents for over ten years.

Tonight, my Cinderella journey ends.

THEY ARE TAKING THE CHILDREN

1980

Mamá turns her head towards us, a worried look on her face. "They are taking the children," she whispers.

Lissette, Rene, and I give her a questioning look. "She must be exaggerating," I tell myself. Then my thoughts shift to my house on Zapote Street.

I wonder what my boyfriend will do when he hears I'm gone. I wish I could have said goodbye. He deserves it, always so attentive with my family. When my little cousin became ill and didn't have *malanga* for a soup, he brought her some. My Tia Pilar thought a soup with malanga would help cure her daughter's stomach, and it did. I miss him already.

I wonder how my aunt feels about us leaving. I imagine her at our empty home, sitting on our bed, buried in thought. I wish she could bring me all the journals I'd written through the years. I don't want her to read them and see how messed up I am.

I decide to focus on my surroundings.

The room in the processing center where the guards take us is packed with families, but no one seems as scared as my mother.

"You see that girl behind the glass-enclosed room?" Mamá says. "You see the uniformed guard? Just a few minutes ago, she was crying. That guard came over to her family and asked her to come with him. This is the second time he has done this since we arrived. The first girl has not been returned to her family."

"They can't do that," I say, acting as if I know everything because I turned fifteen.

"I miss my friends, Mami" my sister, age thirteen, says with tearful eyes. "I don't want to go." Part of me doesn't either. Cuba is all I've known, with its virtues and flaws. Then, there's another part of me that wants to be with Papá and get away from the fiasco my country has become. Nothing makes sense: the ration cards that limit the food we can buy, the control by the government of every business, the

16

dependency on the Soviet Union, the whole idea of communism. I'm not wired that way, which makes my mother giggle, saying that Castro, in his effort to make me a good socialist, created a capitalist. Based on what my mother tells me about capitalism, it makes sense. Those who work hard will see the fruits of their labor. In Cuba, doctors and engineers live like everyone else, so many stopped caring.

"Lissette, wipe those tears right away!" my mother says in a firm voice. Lissette glares at her and wipes her face.

A man wearing a white coat and thick glasses walks towards us. I sense he's trying to remain inconspicuous, but never more than when he stops in front of Mamá and whispers, "Can you come with me?"

"I'm not going anywhere without my children."

"You can bring them."

My mother raises a brow.

"I want to help you," he says, noticing my mother's look. He then scans the room without moving his head, before he returns his attention to Mamá. "Trust me."

She grabs my brother and sister by their hands and asks me to stay close. We follow the man through a long corridor. At the end of the hallway, he opens a door and asks us to come inside an office. On his desk is a picture of a woman, him, and three children. Before he sits behind it, he tells my mother, "Be careful. When officers catch children crying, they take them away to a room and convince them to stay."

His words take me by surprise. I look down and play with my fingers.

"I can help you," he adds, leaning back on his chair and opening a desk drawer. "There are some pills to keep them calm."

I stare at him with defiance.

"I don't want any pills!" I say.

The doctor glances at me with a tranquil expression and leans forward.

"Let me explain something to you. You're leaving everything you know, and your mother is taking you to a strange place. It's natural to feel nervous. I can give you a small dose of Meprobamato to help you relax."

"I'm not taking anything," I said. Lissette and Rene echo my statement.

Mamá notices the picture on the desk.

"Are those your kids?" she asks the doctor.

"Yes. Do you understand now why I want to help you? Besides, I'm a doctor. It's my duty."

"My husband is in the United States, you know. The government kept us apart for twelve years. I need to reunite my children with their father."

"I know," he says.

My mother examines him. Then I notice her expression of distrust disappearing.

"Children, do what the doctor says."

He takes a bottle from his desk drawer, opens it, and gives each of us a small pill.

I take it, wondering if they will make me feel like a zombie. Mamá has taken them for years for her nerves. Almost everyone in Cuba takes them. People say it helps them cope with life here.

My mother thanks the doctor, and we return to the processing room where my paternal grandmother awaits.

"Where did you go?" she asks.

"I'll explain later," my mother replies.

Mamá asks us to pull our chairs closer to her, and we make a semi-circle around her. She leans forward.

"Listen to me very carefully," she says. "You will not mess this up for me. You will not cry. You will not give these men a reason to take you away. I have worked too hard in my life to take you out of Cuba. Today is the day you become men and women. Understood?"

I have never seen her so serious before. The intensity in her eyes would have persuaded anyone to obey. We remain silent.

"Do I make myself clear?" she asks.

We all nod.

"Good."

From outside our semicircle, my grandmother, who had dozed off, opens her eyes and gives me a questioning look. I shrug.

My mother continues to watch the officers at the processing center like a tigress. It's not until much later, when we board a bus, that she relaxes. Outside, hundreds have gathered to yell at us. Mom tells us it is a government-organized protest. People are throwing rocks at the bus and yelling obscenities. Some hold signs with derogatory terms like worms or traitors.

"Don't mind them," Mamá says. "They wish they were here."

We're taken to a camp called *El Mosquito*. We stand in line waiting our turn. A couple women sitting behind a table order us to empty our pockets and remove our jewelry.

"This is a graduation gift from my mother," Mamá tells the woman. "I won't give it to you."

"You have no choice," she says.

"My mother is dead now. This is the only thing I have left of her."

"It makes no difference to me."

"In that case, call your supervisor."

Frustrated, the woman gets up and walks towards my mother.

"Raise your arms. Let me make sure you're not hiding anything in your bra."

Mamá obeys but holds on to her ring. The heavy-set woman pats her down and feels under my mother's breasts.

"I don't have anything in my bra," she says.

"I need to make sure," the woman replies, but by her air of superiority and her smirk, this is payback.

My mother appears embarrassed by the way the woman touches her.

"You can go now," the woman says when she's done.

"And my ring?"

"Go before I change my mind."

My blood boils. I should have slapped the government worker for doing what she did. Instead, I glare at her before walking away.

For three days, we stay at what I term "Concentration Camp *El*

19

Mosquito." Here I learn about hunger. It stabs like a knife and makes me feel weak.

"Keep drinking water," my mother says. "It will fool your body into thinking you're full."

I drink warm water from a rusted faucet. It doesn't help. My stomach hurts so much I may pass out, but I don't. After a while, I get numb to the pain.

There are police dogs everywhere in the camp, so we stay close to Mamá. My sister walks away, and my mother doesn't notice. When she does, she screams, "Where's Lissette?"

I don't know. We look for her everywhere, but there are so many people at the camp, it's hard to see beyond a few feet. My mother's face turns pink, like it does when her blood pressure rises.

"When I see her, I'm going to kill her!" she says pacing back and forth, but I know she doesn't mean it.

At last, we see her in the distance, running towards us, trying to avoid the people in her path. She's crying and red-faced.

"What happened?" my mother asks.

"They bit her!"

"Who?"

"A pregnant woman. The dogs knocked her down and bit her breasts."

I get chills when I hear this. Mamá embraces my sister.

"Don't you ever walk away from me again, you hear?"

"I needed to use the bathroom," my sister replies. "The one here is full of poop!"

My mother tells us she'll take care of the problem. She asks us to stay with my grandmother in the sleeping quarters—an area that looks like a warehouse, with dirt floors and bunk beds. Only the elderly and sick occupy the beds as there aren't enough for everyone, so we must take turns sleeping on a chair.

When Mamá returns, she tells us she has taken care of everything. "If they call us, just follow me. Don't talk to anyone in the group."

We had been assembled in groups upon our arrival. The entire group was scheduled to leave at the same time. However, my mother can be persuasive.

Later, she tells me that after my grandmother's collapse from the lack of food and my sister's incident with the dog, she couldn't risk staying at the camp longer. She asked to speak to someone in charge and told him, "I will kill you if something happens to any of my kids." She uses that term a lot for someone who has the kindness of Mother Teresa and is always taking the little we have and sharing it with others.

Not this time.

At first, he laughed at her. Then she told him her story, and he offered to help.

A few hours later, close to midnight, we line up by a shrimp boat while an officer calls names off a list he reads with the help of a lantern. The woman in front of us carries a baby in her arms, and when her turn arrives, the officer takes it from her.

"You leave; your baby stays," he says.

My mother grabs the hands of my brother and sister and asks me to stay close.

"They will have to kill me," she whispers. "No one is taking my kids."

The woman in front of us cries and begs for her baby. The officer pushes her onto the boat, as I feel a knot in my stomach. Before he calls our names, he asks us to get into the boat one by one.

"Not until everyone has been called," my mother says.

He shines his flashlight on her face.

"Please don't make my kids get on the boat without me. We all have to leave together," Mamá says on the verge of tears.

He hesitates for a moment and begins to read. My brother and my sister are called first. My mother grabs my hands. I feel the coldness of hers. My mother's name is called next, then my grandmother's, then he pauses. I can hear Mamá breathing faster.

At last, the officer calls my name, and we get on the boat.

REUNION

1980

After our boat docks and people disembark, men and women with eyes full of tears fall to their knees and kiss the ground as American soldiers, nuns from the Catholic Church, and workers from the Red Cross greet us with wide smiles.

This is not how I imagined it would be. For years, the Cuban government had taught us at school about the evil American empire, and now, a different reality stands before me.

Mamá embraces us after she notices the American flag floating from a tall flagpole in the distance.

"You see?" she says. "This is why I sacrificed so many years of my life. This is the Land of the Free."

We walk towards the processing center as instructed—a large rectangular metal structure—when my mother stops and turns around, red-faced, muscles tensed.

"Where's your grandmother?"

We look at the people around us but can't find her. Mamá grows restless as our search continues. Moments later, my brother cries, "There she is. She's being carried out of the boat on a stretcher!"

Our heads turn in the direction of the boat, and when I see her body, I think the worst. My eyes focus on her head and hands—the only areas of her body not covered by a blanket—hoping to see her move. Is she alive?

People walk past us, and we stay in place waiting for the stretcher to reach us.

"Abuelita!" my brother yells and waves his hand. She turns her head and when she sees us, she returns the wave. She looks pale and weak.

We later learn that she had become dehydrated during the journey. After she is treated, she joins us at the processing center, where officers interview Mamá before giving us our refugee papers.

By the time we receive them, it is already April 28, 1980, and we don't look like the people who had arrived hours earlier, as we had cleansed our bodies with the Red Cross' toiletries and changed into clothes that people from Miami and other US cities had donated to those arriving to Key West.

That same day, a large bus transports us to a hotel in Miami. We would stay there for two days, courtesy of the church. It is there, as we stand in line, wide-eyed, each carrying a plastic bag full of donated clothes, that a stranger approaches my mother and asks her if she needs help.

How did he know? Why did he pick *her* among the crowd?

She explains to him that my father is still in Cuba waiting for us. "He doesn't know we left on another boat. Can you help me get a message to him?"

The elegant and perfumed stranger promises he will contact the number my mother hands him, gives her twenty dollars she reluctantly accepts, and disappears into the crowd that walks up and down the street in front of the hotel.

"He's an angel God sent to us," my mother says, as her emotions run down her face.

Days later, we walk outside an apartment complex on Biscayne Bay that is scheduled for demolition. Cuban refugee families, needing a temporary place to stay, were taken here. We still have not seen our father, and my mother has started to wonder if we will see him again. In the meantime, we walk, like we do every afternoon, to watch the sunset over the bay. That is when we see a gray car enter the complex and drive through the empty parking lot. My mother asks us to get close to her.

The car parks a few feet from us. The driver's door opens, and a thin, tanned man with a big smile greets us. My mother lets out a scream and runs to him. The kisses and desperate hugs they exchange make me feel awkward.

They stop hugging for a moment and turn towards us.

"Come say hello to your father," Mamá says.

We obey. His eyes glisten as he embraces each one of us and kisses our cheeks. My sister and I give him a cautious glance, but my brother grabs his hand, raises it, and yells with joy. "Yay! I finally have a dad!" We then walk together towards the water to watch the sunset.

LEAVING HOME

1983

Lissette and I sit on the bottom of the bunk bed we share, and she exclaims, "You what?"

It's Friday, October 7, a few months after we graduated from Jefferson High School, in Tampa, Florida.

By now, I'm attending the University of South Florida under a full scholarship. The algebra class is held in a large auditorium with over one-hundred students and the professor stands far away, down at the bottom of the auditorium. I have a hard time understanding my professors and feel this will be a tough year.

My high school experience taught me much about my new home, so different than Cuba where I wore a uniform to school and, for the most part, everyone liked the same music. At Jefferson, some girls wore brand name clothing to school; others wore all black; while others, like me, wore clothes that had been worn by someone else and belonged to the previous decade. Divisions also existed among kids who listened to rock, new wave, punk, rap, salsa, and country music.

One day, while attending a chemistry class, the teacher asked that we break into groups. I was the last one to be assigned, which made me feel awkward. The American kids looked at me as if saying, "I don't want that dummy with me," so I ended up in a group composed of South American kids and new Cuban arrivals. The Cuban kids whose families had come prior to the 1970s also stayed away from the "new arrivals." Those who rejected me didn't realize that chemistry was one of my strongest subjects, and I knew all the elements of the periodic table. In my broken English, I answered all the questions correctly, and my group won. After that day, all the Americans and "old" Cubans wanted me in their group, except that I no longer needed them to choose me.

We live on LaSalle Street, the first house my parents purchased at my mother's insistence. She tells me home ownership is the first step to financial independence. She hides money from my father and sends it to the mortgage company. "When he least expects it, the house will be paid off," she tells me. That's her dream.

Ivan Viamontes and I have been dating since October 1982. He is one of the few "old Cubans" who never rejected me, even when he didn't know I was smart. Over the summer of 1983, after we finish high school, he proposes to me, but my parents insist I'm too young to know what I want. My father tells me I'll not be getting married until he says so. His house, his rules. I wonder what he'll do when he hears the news.

"It was an accident. I didn't mean to," I tell Lissette.

"You're in so much trouble! When Mamá finds out, she'll kill you."

Lissette does the sign of the cross, opening her eyes wide, while trying to contain her giggles. She hasn't changed much over the years, except for her thinner body and long, brown hair that boys like. The beautiful Chinese eyes she inherited from a distant relative have not changed, except that now they are brought to life by my mother's eyeliner. I'm eighteen now, and she just turned seventeen in July, but she's still a child at heart. In many ways, she has also been my light, the only person, other than Ivan, who makes me laugh.

I'm wearing my colorful nightgown that matches my sister's, and I think that I'm the worst person in the world. Only that would explain what I've done. I think about Abuela. If she were here, she could defend me, she could explain that mistakes happen, but she's dead now. It wasn't an illness that ended her life. It was far worse. I still see her when I close my eyes: on the bathroom floor, the gun by her side, and so much blood.

I couldn't let Papá see her like that because during the years he spent without us, alcohol became his shelter. So, the day I found Grandma in the bathroom, I ran out and called 911.

"Whatever you do Papá, don't go in the bathroom," I told him.

He never did. I knew if he had seen what I saw, he would never be able to unsee it. It would have haunted him for the rest of his life, and his drinking would get worse. Me? I'm used to it and have come to expect it. "One way or another, one day everyone will leave me," I told myself. So, I decided it's better if I don't love anyone. That way, I wouldn't get hurt anymore.

Someone knocks on the door.

"Girls, can I come in?" It's my mother's voice.

"Yes," said my sister in an unconvincing way.

Mamá enters the bedroom, and my sister jumps out of the bed and rushes to the corner of the small room, behind my mother. She starts waving her arms to signal that I'm in trouble. Mamá sees her from the corner of her eye.

"What's going on?"

"Nothing," I say looking down.

I'm a horrible liar. Mamá can see right through me.

"Tell me this very moment what the two of you are up to."

"Me?" Lissette says, placing her hands on her hips. "Why do you have to blame me for everything? I'm a little angel with wings."

Mamá's attention turns to me.

"What are you hiding?"

I evade her eyes.

"I didn't mean to, Mamá. It was an accident."

"You didn't mean to do *what?*"

I know if I tell her, my world will come to a halt and hers will too. My breathing accelerates. I feel dizzy. If I could close my eyes and wake up the next morning to find out none of this is happening, I would be so happy.

"If I tell you, will you keep it to yourself and not tell Papá?"

"Tell me what?"

She sits next to me.

"I'm your mother. You can tell me anything."

"Please don't tell Papá."

She grabs my hands—they are ice cold—and gives me a reassuring look. I close my eyes for a moment and look down as I tell her, "I'm pregnant."

Bolting out of the bed, she stands in front of me and yells, "You what?"

I start crying. "I'm sorry. It was an accident."

"An *accident*? You call getting pregnant an accident?" She interlaces her fingers over her bleached blond hair. "Oh my God! How am I going to tell this to your father? This will destroy him, just like it's destroying me."

She pauses for a moment and shakes her head.

"Of all my children, I never expected *you* to do this. You have just thrown your life away."

If I felt bad before, now I'm reduced to a particle of dust. I feel less than nothing. I never intended to hurt her, not her. She doesn't deserve this.

"I'm sorry, Mamá." That's all I can say.

She paces back and forth in the tiny room, arms over her head. Her face reddens as she walks.

"I can't hide this from your father. I can't! I have to tell him."

"Please, Mamá. Don't tell him," I say.

"I can't handle this alone. Not this," she pauses and looks into my eyes with so much pain reflected on her face that all I can do is weep. "Beatriz Valdes, you have killed me today," she says before turning around and exiting the room.

My sister no longer laughs.

"Oh my God," she says and sits next to me.

Moments later, we hear loud voices outside. It's my parents. They are arguing in the cemented patio, just outside our window. My sister turns off our bedroom light, and we peek out through our curtain. We see my father with a bottle of liquor in his hand. "I will kill that son-of-bitch," he says. He keeps drinking, and I feel a tight knot in my stomach.

"He's acting crazy!" I whisper to my sister, and we look at each other before our eyes return to what's happening outside. He's now holding a gun.

"I'm going to kill him!" he yells.

As if I had been hit by lightning, I spring into action.

"I can't stay," I whisper. "I need to leave this house now!"

"Leave where?" my sister says.

"I don't know. I have to leave."

I hug my sister and tiptoe out of the room like a flash until I make it to the street. I still hear the yelling and wonder what the neighbors must be thinking. I need to get as far away as possible. Wearing my striped nightgown and flip flops, I run on the dark street, not knowing where to go, while tears cloud my vision. After running about a block, I see the house of an elderly woman who talks to me once in a while after I return from school. I run to her door and knock several times until she opens.

"I need your help," I say. "I need to call my boyfriend. My father wants to kill him."

She lets me into her small, but well-kept home. After I explain what happened, she allows me to make a telephone call.

My hands shake when I dial Ivan's number. His mother, Madeline, picks up.

"Can I talk to Ivan?" I say as my voice cracks.

"Is everything okay?" she asks.

"I need Ivan to pick me up. I ran away. My dad is angry. Please put him on the phone."

"Oh my God!" she says and pauses. For the next few seconds, I hear her muffled voice, as if she has covered the transmitter portion of her handset. Her voice then becomes clear again. "Of course, sweetheart. Here he is."

I speak to Ivan for only a few seconds, and then his mother picks up the telephone again.

"What happened?" she asks. "He took his car keys and ran out the door."

"My dad says he's going to kill him for getting me pregnant."

"Did he say that? He's probably bluffing, but please tell Ivan not to confront your father. You can come to my house. Don't worry. Everything is going to be okay. Where are you?"

"At a neighbor's house, about a block away."

"Please be careful. I'll pray for you and Ivan. We'll get through this."

After I hang up, Elsa, the elderly woman, asks me to sit on the sofa.

"Let me bring you a glass of water," she says and walks towards the back of the house.

She's gone for a while, while I look at the pictures in her living room, most of her and her husband, who I remember is deceased. After she returns, she sits next to me and watches me drink the water.

"Everything is going to be okay," she says, taking the glass after I'm done.

We talk for a while, before we hear the siren of an emergency vehicle. Then horrible thoughts run through my mind. "Please God. Help me," I say and close my eyes, while Elsa caresses my hands.

"You will be safe here," she says.

The minutes that follow go slow. When we see the lights of a vehicle park in her driveway, she whispers, "Stay here. Let me see who it is. What's your boyfriend's name?"

"Ivan," I say.

Elsa leaves me and moments later returns with Ivan. He rushed to me, and we hug, while tears cloud my vision.

"I thought you were dead," I said.

"I'm okay, my love. I'm okay. Let me take you home."

BECOMING A MOM

Ivan and I get married by a judge with his secretary as the witness. No one attended the ceremony, my mother-in-law Madeline and my father-in-law Guillermo had to work. My parents had to work too, but my father also says that after I left the house, I am dead for everyone. He prohibits any communication with me for months, although Mamá sometimes calls me from her job.

That Christmas, I feel lonely.

The months pass by quickly. I work at Winn Dixie and Ivan at Montgomery Wards' warehouse. A few days after my ninth month of pregnancy, my contractions begin. I sit on the bed and bend my upper body over my lap until I can't take the pain anymore, so I stand up hoping it will get better. It's past midnight, and Ivan is sound asleep after a long day at the warehouse.

"It's hurts so much!" I cry. My voice awakens him.

"What? What?"

"It hurts!"

He rubs his eyes, gets out of bed, and rushes to me.

"What should I do?" he asks, turning on the bedroom lamp.

Suddenly, a copious amount of water falls on the floor, and I don't know what's happening.

"What's that?" he asks while trying not to step on the liquid.

"I don't know! Call your mom."

Ivan runs out of our bedroom. When he returns with her, she doesn't seem as alarmed as Ivan and I are. "Ivan, it's nothing serious. Her water broke. Son, get her bag and drive her to the hospital. The baby is coming."

I wonder if I'm ready for this.

"Can you call my mom and tell her?" I ask Madeline. She smiles, as if sensing my nervousness, and nods in agreement.

I haven't seen my family since the night I left. During this time, my father hasn't spoken to me. No one has, other than my mother.

As Ivan drives over the speed limit to Tampa General Hospital, I wonder if my father will come with my mother to the hospital or ignore the birth of his grandson, as he has ignored me. Mom still doesn't drive and must depend on him for everything.

When we arrive, hospital staff does not appear as concerned as we are, and it takes about fifteen or thirty minutes before a bed becomes available. I'm taken to a room already occupied by two other women who are in various stages of the labor process, each of them in a bed, and each of them screaming when the contractions come. Soon, I join them. I am the youngest of the women and don't know what to expect. The three of us are separated by curtains that are not fully closed.

Nurses come and go, ask me questions, and place monitoring equipment on my body. That's when Ivan starts asking me questions.

"What's that cable for?"

"What's that monitor for?"

At first, I keep my composure, but as my contractions get closer, his questions become increasingly unbearable. After a couple of hours, I've had enough.

"Stop asking questions!" I scream as if I were possessed or had lost my mind. "This is all your fault!"

"Why is it my fault?"

"And you dare to ask? It hurts so much!"

"What should I do?" he asks with a confused expression.

"Go outside and see if your mom and my parents are here!" I shout.

He kisses me on my sweaty forehead before exiting the room. After he leaves, I'm embarrassed to keep screaming, so when the next contraction comes, I close my fists and bury my nails in my hand. Then I notice the torn wallpaper next to my bed. I grab the loose wallpaper and start tearing it off the wall.

Twenty minutes later, Ivan returns with my mother and Madeline, Ivan's mother. When I see my mother, I can't contain my emotions and tears roll down my face. It has been so long.

"Mamá, it hurts," I say.

She embraces me, filling my face with her kisses.

"It will be okay, *mija*. This is part of being a mom," she says and caresses my hair and my face.

"How far apart are the contractions?" Madeline asks.

"Still far," I say.

"You should probably do a C-section. You are so thin to deliver a baby. You barely weighed ninety-eight pounds when you arrived at my house," Madeline replies.

My mother glances at Madeline. "When she was home, she never liked to eat very much, no matter how much I insisted."

"The same thing at my home, so we buy her whatever she likes because she's been eating for two. She's gained thirty pounds during her pregnancy, but she's still too thin."

My mother turns her head towards me, and our eyes meet. Hers appear apologetic. She doesn't have to say anything. I know she did the best she could when her life stopped being hers.

"I missed you so much," she says.

Mamá sits next to me and holds my hand. Then the next contraction comes, and I begin to scream. Tears roll down her face.

"It will be over soon, sweetheart," Mamá tells me.

A nurse comes into the room to check on us. When she sees Ivan, Madeline, and my mother, she shakes her head.

"I already explained that only one family member can be here. Two of you need to go outside."

"Could you please let us stay here? I haven't seen my daughter for several months. This is her first baby, and she's scared."

The nurse takes a deep breath.

"Five more minutes, then two of you must go outside. And one more thing, when you do, please make sure your family stops asking us questions. We are very busy."

When the nurse leaves the room, my eyes turn to my mother.

"Who's here?"

"Everybody," she says.

"Who?"

"Your sister, your brother, your dad, and your in-laws, Madeline and Guillermo, with their twin boys," she replies.

"My dad?" I ask.

She nods. We exchange glances but don't say anything. After a long silence, Madeline says, "We should go."

"You're right," my mother replies. "Ivan, you stay here with Betty. I will be right outside, in the waiting area. Ivan will come get me if you need me. Okay?"

"Yes, Mamá. Thank you for coming."

Hours pass and all the women around me have left and new ones have taken their place, but my baby refuses to leave my womb. A nurse comes in and informs me that she plans to give me a medication that will speed up my contractions. She also says, "Your family is disturbing the nurses. Either they stop, or they will be asked to leave."

"What are they doing?" I ask.

"Requesting status reports every five minutes," she says, "especially, the blond lady."

Her comments make me laugh as I imagine my mother.

"It's not funny," she said.

"I know. I'm sorry. My husband will go outside and ask them to be patient."

She thanks us. Once she gives me the medication and it takes effect, my contractions come more frequently. I am so tired, but a nurse tells me I'm almost there. Ivan is not in the room since he is talking to the family. Suddenly, another nurse comes in.

"Whatever you do, do not push," she tells me, and the two nurses start wheeling me away.

Not push? Have they lost their minds? I have been in labor for twenty-one hours, so all I want is to deliver this baby. I don't listen and push. I can't take this pain any longer.

By the time I get to the operating room, there is no time. I feel the cut of the blade and the blood from the episiotomy roll down. Moments later, something warm and slippery comes out of my body. The obstetrician wraps the baby in blankets, but I am too tired to see what else she does. That's when I hear the baby cry. It's like soft music to my ears.

"It's a beautiful baby boy. Congratulations! Do you want to hold him?"

After so many hours, I feel exhausted.

"Yes," I say with a faint voice, my face shiny with sweat.

She places him in my arms and stays by my side.

"Hello, little boy," I say and kiss his cheeks, but I don't have the strength to hold him.

"I can't" I say, and a nurse takes him from me.

The notion that I am now a mother and am responsible for this tiny being hits me. If I don't know how to care for myself, how can I care for him? I close my eyes, and by the time I open them, I'm in a different room with Ivan by my side and the baby in his arms.

"Where is everybody?" I ask.

"The nurse is bringing them now."

"Is Dad still here?"

"Yes."

A few moments later, the room is invaded by family, each taking a turn holding the baby, but my father has stayed by the entrance of the room without saying a word. After a while, my mother notices.

"Ray? Come on over to meet your grandson."

All eyes turn to him, as he nervously walks towards my mother who holds the baby. My mother places my son in his arms.

"Little Ivan, this is your grandpa Ray," my mother says with a little girl's voice.

My father looks at the baby and then at me. His eyes glisten, and he wipes a tear that has rolled down his face.

OUR EARLY YEARS OF MARRIAGE

1985-1992

The first years of marriage have been unlike anything I expected. So many fights, so many arguments driven by our frustrations and the realization that we are on our own. Nothing has been easy. We have been living in a trailer off Sheldon Road since Ivan Jr was three months old. Ivan is still working at the warehouse, and me at Centro Español Hospital as a receptionist, a job I found right after my son was born, thanks to my mother's contacts at the hospital.

Three years ago, in 1985, Hurricane Elena came very close to Tampa, so close that a tornado lifted our shed in the middle of the night and threw it into our neighbor's shed. We should have evacuated as recommended by the weather service. We could've died that night. Our female finch did. She became so nervous when our trailer started to shake, she died of a heart attack. I can only imagine what would have happened if the hurricane had come on land.

After realizing we could not spend another hurricane season living in the trailer, we bought a tiny three-bedroom-one-bathroom home that had been remodeled after a fire. It was so hard to save the small down payment. At the beginning, I had to hide money from Ivan. He was so used to buying records and music equipment. Now, that has changed. He gives me his entire check. We make our lunches every day and don't buy new clothes very often.

We visit our parents every week, but it has been difficult for me to love anyone. I don't want to get hurt again. I loved my father when he lived in Cuba, and he left. I loved my mother, and she attempted against her life. At fifteen, I had fallen in love, and that too ended when I left Cuba. My grandmother then succeeded in taking her life. It's probably safer for those around me if I don't love them. That's what I told myself. That's what I told Ivan. "Honey, I enjoy your company most of the time, except when we fight, but don't expect me to love you. I'm not capable of loving." Even after my son was born, although I knew I would do anything to keep him safe, I refused to call that love.

I called it responsibility.

My mother keeps asking me to hug her and show her affection. I can't.

When Ivan and I first moved to the trailer, we lived off credit cards for a full year. I knew we had to find a way out, or our relationship would not survive. I also knew going back to his mother's house was not an option. It would be an admission of failure. Obtaining an education was the only answer.

It's 1988 now, and we're both attending college. Ivan goes to Tampa Technical Institute and me to Hillsborough Community College. Our fights have ended for the most part. There is no time. We work full time. Ivan goes to class five nights a week after finishing at the warehouse. I've alternated between a full time and half-time schedule at the college, also after work. Sometimes, I wish I could be like those mothers who have the option of staying home. Our son is growing up so fast, and I'm missing it, but I have no choice.

My goal is to send him to private school when he finishes the sixth grade. Some people in my family laugh at me. "You hardly have enough for you, and you want to send him to private school?" I will show them how. Their laughter has turned into my determination.

MY FATHER

1996-1997

D ad glances at those who have gathered with him today to celebrate his fifty-ninth birthday. It's the third Saturday of February 1996. As we sit at the beautiful Columbia Restaurant near Clearwater Beach overlooking the expanse of blue intracoastal waters, I can only imagine what he's thinking when he glances at Ivan, Jr. who will turn twelve in April. He tells me that Ivan Jr. is his pride and joy, although I'm sure he shares a similar comment with my sister about her two boys. Dad is surrounded by his three children, three grandchildren, two sons-in-law, a daughter-in-law, and my in-laws, and life is great.

I finished my bachelor's in business administration—and I'm working on a master's in accountancy—from the University of South Florida, becoming the first person in my family to graduate from college. I kept a perfect grade point average on my masters, even though I worked full time and attended classes in the evening, like I have been doing since my son turned four. That's what I must do to send my son to private school and give him the life I wish I could've had.

My husband has been by my side for thirteen years, working days and studying in the evening, which doesn't leave a lot of time for our son. I hope Ivan Jr. understands we do this for him, for the life we want him to live. He stays with my parents when I attend college, but sometimes, when Mom and Dad work late, I have to take him to class at the university.

Last year, I was hired at Tampa General Hospital as an accounting manager. I love my job and the beautiful four-bedroom house we purchased in Carrollwood, big enough to accommodate our frequent family gatherings. In December 1995, we held Christmas at my house for the first time

Today, something about my father seems off. Perhaps, it's the way he looks around, lost in thought, when he has always been the life of the party. Dad has lived a rough life. He was left at an orphanage when he was nine years old, shortly after his older brother and father died. My grandmother thought the priests at the orphanage would do a better job raising a boy than she could. Dad begged to be taken out of the orphanage, but he didn't leave until he was seventeen. After that, all he wanted was a family. He eventually met my mother, and the two of them had three children, one after another. Castro came to power a few years before we were born and declared Cuba's alliance to the Soviet Union. That's when my mother told my father we needed to leave Cuba.

Dad was to leave first, which he did in 1968, when I was three years old. Then in 1970, Castro stopped allowing people to leave the island, and my father lost his children for twelve years. All he dreamed of when he lived at the orphanage was to have a big family.

It's taken many years, heartache, and tears, but at last, my father has achieved his dream of a big, united family.

That night, when he and Mom return home, he tells her he doesn't feel well, but he goes on about his business. He works at a shop behind the house, a dusty place he built himself, where he cuts the glass for mirror walls he installs in houses and business establishments, even strip bars—Dad doesn't discriminate. It is in the shop where he creates the swans and vases he sells while smoking pack after pack of Moore Menthols. All the years smoking led to his emphysema. Mom tells me a recent test revealed he had the lungs of an eighty-year old, but he won't stop. He's hard-headed like me.

When my mother calls me a few days later, I am not ready for what I hear from the other side of the telephone.

"Hurry! The ambulance just took your father to the hospital."

"What's wrong with him?" I ask.

"A stroke."

Until then, I had never come to terms with the notion that one day, I would lose my parents.

My father spends several days at Tampa General Hospital. He's sent home in a wheelchair, unable to speak. Overnight, my father becomes a shadow of the man he was. Every time he sees an elderly driver, he points at him or her and at his useless legs. He then places his index finger against his temple, as if it were a gun.

"You have to keep trying, Dad! You can't give up!" I tell him.

It hurts me to see him so helpless. Even more ironic is that although my father cannot speak or walk, he is able to sing one song, *Ave Maria*, which never fails to make us cry because he lost his faith in God when his mother left him at the orphanage.

Dad turned 60 in March of 1997, and not much has changed. He is still in a wheelchair. He still can't speak. Mom now takes care of their small business. She hired my sister's husband, and my father, from his wheelchair, shows him what to do. My mother has learned how to measure the jobs and is great at finding new customers, so little by little, my father is replaced. His life becomes monotonous as he sits in front of a television set day after day, or my brother-in-law helps my mother carry him around the house. This is not the life Dad envisioned.

My father would not see Christmas of 1997. Another stroke claims his life before Thanksgiving.

MY MOTHER

2001-2011

In 2001, almost four years after my father passed away, the news that my mother had six months to live unravels me. The doctors tell us she has a rare form of cancer called carcinoid tumors. I tell myself, "No, she can't die. I'm not ready." Not that I will ever be.

I still work at Tampa General Hospital where miracles happen every day, and I need my own miracle. I feverishly research her condition in the middle of the night, after a day of work and night classes at the university.

Not much is known about her disease and after two reams of research pile on my desk at home, I find a glimmer of hope. Some patients with carcinoids of the intestines are showing improvement with Sandostatin injections, except that no one has used Sandostatin for carcinoids of the lungs. It's a long shot, I know, but I bring my research to her doctor. Her young doctor smiles at me with compassion.

"Betty, this treatment has never been tried on patients with carcinoid of the lungs," he says.

"But what if it works? Wouldn't you do everything if she were your mother?"

His smile attempts to conceal the sadness in his eyes. I would learn later that his mother had just lost her life to cancer.

"Fine," he tells me. "I will try."

Days later, after her insurance approves the $1,000-per-month treatments, the injections begin. A day after the first one, she starts breathing better, and a couple of months later, she can function longer and longer without oxygen. But no matter how much she's improving, she still thinks she's going to die.

"Hurry!" she tells me. "We need to document my story."

Since our arrival from Cuba, she has been telling me that I must write a book about our lives. "The world cannot forget what happened to the Cuban people," she says.

41

Yet, I'm always so busy. I have several pages written, but the book is far from over.

"Okay, Mom. Let's do it."

I start to write feverishly, and she does too, in journals or single sheets of paper, afraid her time will run out. She still misses my father so much, always looking at the pictures of his grandchildren and him. His grandchildren were his life. His smile was never as broad as when he spent time with them. I think his death contributed to Mamá's condition.

"You must fight for your life, Mamá," I tell her. "You did all you could for him."

Each Christmas she remains alive, I'm so thankful.

The passage of time grows the family, as a set of twins, a boy and a girl, my brother's first children, come into the world. Well, that's what we thought back then. Years later, Mamá would learn my brother had fathered a daughter during his teenage years. And then, another daughter would surface from the time my brother and his wife were divorced and before they decided to remarry.

All of the drama in the family, plus my mother's small glass business, keep her entertained. The twins, and later, Amber, the daughter my brother fathered as a teenager, give her a reason to stay alive.

Meanwhile, I finish my master's in business administration at the University of South Florida (USF) with almost straight A's and get promoted to director of accounting.

I love the university and don't want to stop learning. I see the benefits of my education as my pay continues to increase to levels I never imagined. This allows me to help my mother and siblings and take my mother on trips to Mexico and Europe. She travels to Europe with a small group of women and sends me a picture of her standing in front of the lit Eiffel Tower. She is in front of it pointing up, a big smile adorning her face, while her black jacket wears the falling snow.

After the MBA, I decide to go back to USF and obtain a graduate certificate in creative writing. This knowledge will allow me to finish my mother's book.

The Sandostatin injections give my mother ten years of life but also take a toll on other aspects of her health. She has developed diabetes. Her uncontrolled weight has done the rest. In 2011, she's done fighting, and although she did get to meet her granddaughter Amber, her only regret is not having met Andrea, the other daughter my brother fathered.

"I will stop the injections," she tells me on the way to her doctor's appointment.

"You can't do that!" I yelled. "You will die."

"Betty, I'm seventy-two. I've lived ten years on borrowed time, and I'm so thankful to God, but look at me. I don't have any quality of life. I'm back to using oxygen. My heart is starting to give up."

"But Mom…"

She smiles and holds my hand, and I feel the tears coming, but I make sure I hold them back.

"What would you like to eat after we leave the doctor?" I ask her to get my mind off the subject.

"Buy me a big breaded steak. That's what I want."

For the first time, I don't tell her this is the wrong food for her.

"Anything you want, Mamá," I say.

A couple of months later, I take her to the second rental property I had purchased. Her breathing is labored, even with the oxygen, but she looks at the interior of the house in awe, as the workers paint it and get everything ready for the renters.

"It's beautiful," she says and holds my hand. "You've done well, Betty. You have made me proud. Now, I can die in peace."

"Stop talking like that," I say.

Her beaming smile says it all. She later gives a laundry list of instructions. She would love for my brother and sister to have a business. She wants us to find her granddaughter Andrea, who was taken out of the country when she was a baby. She wants us to tell Andrea she never stopped looking for her.

A few days later, I am in the office when the Vice President of

Patient Accounting walks in and finds me crying.

"What's wrong?" he asks.

"It's my mom," I say as tears roll down my face. "Someone from the hospital called. She died on her way there, but the ambulance workers brought her back. However, the doctors don't think she has much time left."

"Let me take you there. You're in no condition to drive."

On the way, he remains silent as I call each member of the family and ask them to join me at St Joseph's Hospital.

Mom would never smile or speak again. The doctor says she had suffered a massive heart attack and a stroke. He asks us to let her go. I run out of the room when he says this, but my brother agrees.

Mamá's biggest fear is to die alone. A couple of days after the doctors removed her from life support, she takes her last breath. Her children, my aunt and uncle, her cousin, and my in-laws stand by her side while her daughters hold her hands.

LIFE AFTER MAMÁ

2011-2015

My mother didn't want us to spend money on her, but we give her a celebration of life to remember, along with a long video documenting the happy times, a packed funeral home with many flower arrangements, and several of us speaking in front of the congregation to honor her legacy. On the day of her burial, her body is escorted by police and over thirty cars, first to a Catholic church in Ybor City, where a priest delivers a beautiful service, and then to the cemetery.

After life returns to normal, the importance of preserving my mother's essence takes form. That's when I remember my promise to her. I must finish her story, but I can't read her journals without falling apart. I start and stop dozens of times. Meanwhile, I decide not to sell her house, and instead use it as a rental. It will be a business that all her children can share. She made it clear before she died, "The money from the house is to do with as you wish. It is your money." As a rental, her home will provide a steady stream of money that each of us can use as we wish. Some of us use it for the family or to help people in need, like the time a young man died, and the family didn't have money for a funeral, or the day a woman running away from an abusive marriage needed help. Numerous projects. In each, my mother's essence stayed alive.

As I approach my fiftieth birthday, I realize I cannot wait any longer. I need to finish my mother's book. As hard as it is, I open her journals, and what I discover was invaluable. I realize then that I can't write her story in third person. She has to tell her own story. I have to give her a voice. Then, I start piecing her life together like a puzzle. It is a journey of discovery, a journey that becomes the most difficult task I have ever done, a journey of reclaiming, and reconnecting. One of the biggest challenges in writing her story is understanding the events that took her to the day I came home when I was six, and I learned she was about to take her life.

"Why?"

As good a person as she was, why would she leave three little children alone?

I'm fifty years old and trying so hard to understand why anyone would do that, especially her, who was kindness and love personified. I speak to my aunt and everyone who remembers those times, and then, little by little, the puzzle is unraveled. I read the journals and letters she left me to help me fill the gaps.

As I write, I sense her desperation when she returns from the immigration office in Havana after a government official sexually harassed her. He had offered to help her in exchange for sex. She would never do such a thing. Her belief in God, the lessons she received when she attended a school run by Catholic nuns, and her mother's teachings gave her a strong moral compass that no one could break.

I watch Mamá's sadness when her mother dies at age fifty-seven shortly after my father left. My grandmother Angela had been Mamá's rock, sewing for years to give her daughters a chance at a better life. Even when my grandfather lost the small store he owned to gambling, my grandmother worked day and night to try to lift the family out of poverty.

I feel Mamá's angst when the food she can buy at the grocery store with the ration cards is not enough to feed us.

I feel her sense of loss, not knowing how long it will be before she sees the love of her life again. She fell in love with my father in 1961, when she met him at a window factory in Havana. She had been called to his office for being late on repeated occasions due to her mother's illness. There he was, his leather boots on the table, wearing a smile that stopped her heart. After a few weeks of friendship, she became his confidant. Not knowing how much she loved him, he asked her to select gifts for his fiancée, and she did, never revealing her feelings for him. It wasn't until he realized that the woman he was about to marry could not give him a family that he broke off the engagement. His anger and sadness led him to drive a motorcycle at full speed through

Havana's waterfront, until he crashed it and lost consciousness. When he woke up at a hospital bed and found my mother by his side, praying for him and crying, he realized what he had not been able to see all along. Shortly after, he asked her to marry him.

All she wanted was to be with him for the rest of her life, and now, she doesn't know how long it would be before they see each other again.

I watch how unattended depression fills her with darkness. She must have asked herself how will she be able to care for three little children when she doesn't feel capable of caring for herself?

Not that all of these events excuse her action. Nothing would ever justify someone taking that step, but they help me explain it. Reconstructing her past allows me to understand how desperate she felt that day—

When I finally become *her* through the pages of my book and see her on the day she attempted against her life, I become a sea of tears that won't stop flowing, but I forgive her. And now, I feel so sorry she can't be here to give her all the hugs she asked me to give her that I didn't because I was too broken to understand.

LEGACY

B etween 2011 and 2015, my life is consumed by work, community service, and writing. I have joined the Florida Institute of CPAs Healthcare Conference Committee and help organize an event every year to bring continuing education to Florida CPAs. I speak at various professional gatherings and revert to my years as a child when writing allowed me to cope. Back then, by making up stories of princesses and princes facing doom scenarios, writing helped me keep all that happened inside. Now that Mamá has passed away, writing becomes my shield, especially after my son gets married at the end of 2011. Soon, writing would help me bring it all out.

My son, who by now has completed a master's in business administration at USF and has had a successful career, moves to Hoboken, New Jersey with his wife and starts to work in New York City. That leaves Ivan and me.

Writing and the walls I built to avoid getting too close to anyone help me cope with his departure. I remember telling myself as he was growing up, "Don't get too attached. He too will leave," and when he does, I'm ready and my life goes into overdrive.

I stay busy all the time.

Ivan and I carpool to our jobs, so I write while he drives. It takes us an hour to drive from Odessa.

I write after dinner and in the middle of the night, noticing that I only need five hours of sleep to function. Self-discipline takes me to higher levels of functioning at home and work. By now, I have been promoted multiple times at Tampa General Hospital, the latest promotion takes me from director of a department of thirty individuals to Corporate Controller. I am responsible for the accounting and finance operations of a $1.2 billion, multi-entity, nonprofit organization that contributes in significant ways to the health of our community. But that is not enough for me. My mother would have expected more. That is what I keep telling myself to find new ways to do more for the community I love.

When I was growing up, my mother used to tell me that a *santera*, a woman who practiced Santeria, told her she would have a daughter who would become a famous writer one day. She was always reminding me of that.

"Famous? Me?" I would tell her. "On what planet?"

In the journals my mother left me, it becomes clear she knew the day would come when I would read them. "Betty, I had already told you this part of the story, but not this other part," she wrote. It was as if she were by my side advising me on her story. She also left us several photo albums. One of them was the first picture we took upon our arrival to America. Beneath it, she wrote in Spanish, "Our first picture in the land of the free. Never forget."

Reading her journals and looking through old albums fuel me and lead me to create a publishing company. I learn about publishing, manuscript editing and formatting, character development, marketing, and cover design.

In January 2015, after many tears, long nights, and exhaustion, I finally finish her book, and when I do, a sense of peace envelopes me. I walk around our house looking at all the places where she used to sit, remembering her, imagining her. I get to the family room and find my husband reading a politics book.

"I'm done," I said in a calm tone of voice.

"Already?" he asked. I'm not sure if he's trying to mock me, but his face doesn't seem to suggest it.

"It's been a total of fourteen years on and off."

"That's great! Congratulations!"

He opens his arms towards me and smiles, and I go to him and accept his embrace. After he returns to reading, I walk back towards the front of the house and enter the bedroom where Mamá slept. There is an album on the nightstand with her wedding picture on the front cover, and as I get closer, I see a folded piece of paper sticking out behind the picture, in an opening on the album cover. I pull it out and read:

To my children and grandchildren: I only ask that you love each other and your spouses with the same intensity that united your father and me. It didn't matter the stones we found along the way, the unjust politics, the twelve years of separation. We stayed together until the very end. Love is the greatest feeling that exists in the world.

Love,

Mamá and Papá (till death do us part)

Tears emerge and roll down. For almost four years that note waited to be found, and the fact that I found it when I finished her book conveys a clear message. I must include the wedding picture and her words in the book.

Waiting on Zapote Street, my mother's story, is published on March 2, 2015.

Through word of mouth, the book's readership expands in the United States and internationally. It is selected by a United Nations book club and many others. The Latino Author website lists it as one of the ten best books of 2016, and eventually in 2018, it would win the *Latino Books Into Movies Award,* an award that Edward James Olmos himself would announce.

After the publication, I feel restless. What else would my mother want me to do? What is my purpose? How can I best leave a mark? How can I pay it forward and pay back to this country that opened her arms to us? Those questions drive me. I network with other community leaders looking for that next project that will allow me to give back. I also continue to write and work at Tampa General Hospital.

Finally, through a group of businesswomen and community leaders, I meet one of the assistants of Florida's governor, Rick Scott. When she hears my story, and how education transformed my life, she encourages me to apply to a position at the Board of Trustees of Hillsborough Community College. At the end of 2015, I receive a call from the governor's office. He is flying down to Tampa to meet with me. I can't believe it. The Governor of the State of Florida is coming to meet *me?*

I prepare feverishly for that interview, and when I finally meet him at an airport near Tampa, I cannot believe I'm talking to him. It doesn't take long for him to decide. He tells me I'm the most prepared candidate he has interviewed, and this is "a no-brainer." He then asks the photographer to take a picture with me. And just like that, he appoints me to the Hillsborough Community College Board of Trustees. This appointment represents a huge responsibility—five campuses and over 40,000 students.

By the end of 2016, I'm managing the finances of the hospital and about eleven subsidiaries, including a joint venture. I'm part of the management team that took the hospital from a money-losing organization in 1995 that was thirty days away from closing its door, to becoming a world class profitable organization. I love the hospital, its people, and its mission, but since my appointment, I use most of my vacation time traveling to Tallahassee and Washington D.C. to advocate for Hillsborough Community College and attend education seminars for trustees and other community events.

On one occasion, I attend a holiday celebration at the governor's mansion and speak to the head of the Ways and Means Committee to ask him for $10 million for the Allied Health building for the college. He gives me his business card and asks me to send him an e-mail. I do. When I later learn the college was awarded the $10 million, my excitement about the impact that we, as individuals, can have propels me to take an unprecedented step.

In 2017, the groundbreaking ceremony for the Allied Health building takes place, but I'm unable to attend it because of job commitments. It is difficult for me not to be there to celebrate the hard work the college administrators and staff did to get to that moment. So, after twenty-two years, I decide to devote more time to the community, and I write my resignation letter.

No one at Tampa General Hospital expect this.

Some members of the family ask me, "Who would leave a six-figure plus income in favor of community work?"

I just look at them and don't say anything. By now, we own several

51

rental houses that provide us with decent income. I know after I leave the hospital, we won't be as comfortable as we are now, and we will have to watch our spending more carefully, but I don't hesitate. My decision is made, and I never look back.

To ensure a smooth transition, I give a three-month notice. I hope that will allow the hospital enough time to find a suitable replacement, but no matter what, I assure my boss I am willing to help. That's the least I can do.

In February 2018, I leave Tampa General Hospital. By then, I had finished three other books, *The Dance of the Rose, Candela's Secrets and Other Havana Stories*, and *Havana: A Son's Journey Home*, all bringing to light the struggle of the Cuban people. It is hard work, many long hours, but the comments from my readers, the testimonies of how my books helped them or gave them the strength they needed, motivate me to keep writing. I'm in the middle of writing another book, the story of my in-laws, a book my husband asked me to write after seeing the impact of my other books.

I spend hours sitting with his parents, getting to know them at a deeper level, learning aspects of their lives that not even my husband knows, and what a gift it is to hear their story. Watching them hold hands after over sixty years of marriage invigorates my belief in the power of love. By helping them remember, they seem to be reliving it all. They smile, shed tears, get closer to each other as if they were newlyweds, and sometimes argue when he tells me stories that she thinks are useless, but I find priceless.

In December 2018, after receiving a call from my previous boss about a Tampa General Hospital physician who needs help with his business, I also begin consulting for a luxury hotel, while writing my in-law's story, performing my duties as trustee, and managing my rental business.

By 2019, I feel fulfilled. We have moved to a new house, and I am doing everything I love. That's when I receive another life-changing call. A board member from Lions Eye Institute for Transplant & Research, Inc., who has followed my career for years, wants me to apply for the Chief Financial Officer position at that company.

"I appreciate the offer, but I'm busy doing all the things I love. I'm not interested."

"Please, think about it," he said.

When I start to research the company, I realize this is the same company that called me when my mother passed away to ask me for her eyes. At the time, I couldn't do it. She wasn't an organ donor, but I was also angry to get that call. My reaction bothered me for years. What if her eyes could have helped someone see? Life was giving an opportunity to right a wrong, so I call the board member and tell him enthusiastically that I will apply for the job.

I prepare for the interview for hours, as I hear I will face strong competition.

In April 2019, I become the first female executive of the Lions Eye Institute for Transplant and Research, Inc., a nonprofit organization that gives the gift of sight to people around the world.

In August 2019, I become the Chair of Hillsborough Community College and publish *The Girl from White Creek*, the story of my in-laws, which is featured as the Number One release on Amazon (for its category).

Around the same time, I receive a call from Tampa Hispanic Heritage Inc.

"Betty, you won!" Odette Figueruelo tells me.

"I won what?" I ask. It's late, and I am exhausted. In fact, my husband has already fallen asleep on the sofa.

"You're the 2019 Hispanic Woman of the Year!"

I'm in shock, and the memory of my mother fills me with emotion. I can hardly get a word out, as this is not my award, *it is hers*.

In September, as the new Hillsborough Community College Chair, I speak in representation of the board, and share the stage with a state senator, the mayor, the president of the college, the largest donor in the history of the college, and key campus presidents during the ribbon-cutting ceremony of the Allied Health Building—the building that was started two years prior that will significantly increase the college's ability to provide state of the art training to allied health students. The event is one of the best attended in the college's history, which shows the level of community support. A plaque inside the building captures my name as the Chair and those of other key players who helped make this dream a reality. While I speak, I can't believe I'm here, taking my mother's dreams to new heights.

It is October 5th as I finish my portion of this collaboration with three women who have also had amazing journeys. Since the news of my selection, I have been in numerous television, radio, and newspaper interviews, and in a week, I will be attending the 2019 Tampa Hispanic Heritage, Inc. Woman and Man of the Year gala to receive this award, which will include various proclamations signed by Tampa's Mayor and various senators.

As I look at the road ahead, I realize my job is far from over. I want to keep writing and hope to see my mother's story on the big screen one day. I want to help others realize their dreams.

Recently, I was at a board meeting at the Southshore campus of Hillsborough Community College, and three students shared their stories. Deeply touched by them, I invited them to join me at the gala as my guests. In total, five students will be joining me. I hope that by sharing my story with them, they too will see what's possible, and one day, they will encourage others to become the best version of themselves. Like I told one of the female students, "Tomorrow, I want you to become Hispanic Woman of the Year. You have it within you. You can do it!"

Meanwhile, I'm working arduously at Lions Eye Institute for Transplant and Research, Inc., helping it improve its financial stability so it can expand research, education, and continue to help mothers and fathers see their children's faces and children see the wondrous world.

When I was living in Cuba, I never imagined my life, but somehow, my mother always believed in me, and *she* made me believe.

EPILOGUE

When I first met the other members of Four Island Sisters Publishing in 2019, I didn't know what to expect. We were so different. We were as politically divided as the nation, and yet, somehow, we had to find commonalities among us. We had to respect the others' opinions, reach consensus, and not allow our strong personalities to get in the way of progress. It was hard at times. There were tears, a sense that this wasn't for us, that we needed to stand alone as we had all our lives, but instead, we realized that together we would be able to achieve something greater than our individual selves. Together we would be able to define what it means to live in America and have Hispanic roots. Together we would help others view a portion of their lives in each of our journeys and find themselves, like we had.

And so, we made it work, until together, we found an ocean in the desert.

ACKNOWLEDGMENT AND APPRECIATION

I would like to thank all of the following people for their incredible help in assembling the information that would form the basis of this story:

My mother, for dedicating her life to her family, and for the hours she spent with me after her cancer diagnosis, telling me about her life during the years the Cuban government kept us apart from my father. For the journals and letters she left to me, containing information she did not have time to tell me as the end was coming near.

Maria Fernandez, for the hours spent on the telephone and exchanging e-mails providing information about my mother's life.

My sister, Lissette, for helping me recreate through her memories the events that took place at El Mosquito; and to my brother, Rene, for his encouragement.

My husband, for all his love and support.

The co-authors of this book, for their dedication to this project.

My readers, for their unparalleled support. I will be eternally grateful.

Figure 1 – Havana, Cuba. 1969 Betty, Rene, Lissette, and their mom, Milagros.

Figure 2 – Caribbean Cruise, circa 2009.

REDEFINING

Anna Brubaker

PROLOGUE

Excerpt from "Alone"
Edgar Allan Poe, 1875

From childhood's hour I have not been
As others were—I have not seen
As others saw—I could not bring
My passions from a common spring—
From the same source I have not taken
My sorrow—I could not awaken
My heart to joy at the same tone—
And all I lov'd—I lov'd alone—

I am a child sprung from the branches of many trees. But my trunk, and my roots, grow solitary, on their own, into the ground wherever I make my home.

I am a woman, once a girl, whose trunk grew strong among both silky blossoms and nettled weeds. Though I was surrounded by others, I grew up alone.

I am a mother and a grandmother, a fierce and loving one, rooted on the horizon. I watch with love, stretching my branches in support of the children and grandchildren whose seeds will be buffeted elsewhere by the wind.

I watch them alone.

I am a life partner whose branches wrap around another trunk to cradle against the storm, who shelters behind another when my branches ache and feel ready to snap. Entwined with another, I still remain alone.

I belong to many tribes. The blood of many peoples flows through my veins. I am of them all, yet I am unique, an individual.

I stand alone.

I have changed the names, addresses, locales, and some dates in the story I have to tell. I changed them because in the end, the story is mine and mine alone. It is a story I tell with much love and appreciation for the people in it.

WHAT FATHER SAID

1985

My wedding was set for April 26, 1986. Chernobyl blew up that day.

My life blew up a few months before that.

I'm not a detail person. Keep your spreadsheets and calendars and timelines. Don't get me wrong, I admire people who can organize like that, but if you're wanting a dates-and-numbers person for a project, that's not me.

Yet here I was on a sunny day in October, six months before I was set to say, "I do," handling detail # 1,005, give or take a few, of what I had come to think of as the Great Extravaganza. I was in stealth mode at my desk in a small public relations firm in Ohio... well, actually, the desk was a door laid across two filing cabinets, but my bosses had to start somewhere. I had a few minutes before lunch, and I had a phone—the old-school kind that connected to a socket in the wall. Perfect time to squeeze in a few calls.

I was excited about this wedding.

My groom, whom I'll call Hal for purposes of storytelling, came from precisely the kind of midwestern American family to which I wanted to belong—big, boisterous, Catholic, with very few rules but a lot of great stories. Six siblings all together, including a set of adorable ten-year-old twin girls. Example behavior: the twins were convinced that after all the ruckus of my introduction to the family (which on that night included a couple of curious neighbor kids), their brother and I would seize the opportunity to make out as soon as we were alone in the living room. They hid behind the couch to ensure they missed nothing. They saw nothing, not even one set of limbs akimbo. Their giggles led to a most unceremonious ushering from the room (them, not me).

I learned quickly to grab all the food I wanted from a platter as it came around the first time at my fiancé's family's crowded dinner table during the holidays. There'd likely be little left if the dish came around a second time. So many Christmas presents, it took two or three hours to open them all. Arguments and orders: "He licked my spoon and now it's gross!!" "Get downstairs and clean up that basement. It's a pigsty!" "Why does [insert name of sibling here] get to go to the concert but I don't? This is SO unfair! I hate you all!" Relatives and neighbors dropping by at 2 a.m. to have a beer, or watch a movie, or maybe both. Pies and cakes magically coming from Grandma's house. Weddings, baby showers, First Communion parties, Mass every weekend...

Why did it mean so much to me to join a tribe like this one?

I grew up as a Hoosier princess on my parents' sixty-acre farm in Indiana. I fed baby lambs with milk. I picked wildflowers. I kept frogs in jars. I explored the creek and the orchard and the edge of the forest with my trusty German Shepherd babysitter, a dog who once pawed a snake from my path. I listened to crickets and cows lowing in the barn before I fell asleep each night. My mother called me to dinner in Hungarian every evening. The sparse conversation that made its way around the table at those dinners was also in Hungarian, a language that no one around me but my parents and their friends ever spoke.

Holidays at my house were the three of us around a table with a roast duck in the middle—no aunts, no uncles, no cousins. Three of us, that is, until my father drank himself angry and would storm off, only to pass out on the floor in front of the television later. I always got his portion of flavorless walnut cake.

I didn't invite friends over much.

My first—and last—birthday party, when I turned seven, was a majestic, soaring aria of a failure. My school friends all refused to eat the flavorless walnut cake of Thanksgiving fame, the only cake my mother knew how to make. No games were planned, no party favors, just four kids speaking their truths about the whole setup being the most boring thing they'd ever done in their lives. One asked to use the phone to call her mom to get her when it became obvious the only thing my parents thought happened at *Amerikai* (American) birthday parties was that people ate cake.

I spent a lot of time alone, and I learned early on to amuse myself.

My parents would buy me whatever they could afford—swim and dance lessons, school trips, concert tickets, all the books I could ever want.

They just couldn't buy me a life that felt like anyone else's.

I sound selfish and ungrateful as I say this, I know. But I wanted to be like everyone else, whose mothers could drive, whose parents would come to conference night at school, who could understand the financial aid forms that were required for college. I wanted to quarrel with a brother or sister, or perhaps one of each. Well, really, it wasn't quarrelling that I wanted so much as it was to have someone else with whom to mourn the life I didn't have, who would understand why that life was different than the lives of people born and raised as Americans.

I don't know why I was so stuck on the mantra of American = good, Non-American = bad. I didn't grow up in an era where "foreigners" were demonized as leeches and criminals, as they often are now. Most people in the small Midwestern places where we lived thought it was very cool to be us, the little Hungarian family on the edge of town.

But no one knew what went on behind those proverbial closed doors.

Maybe I thought it would have been easier to step over my father lying passed out on the floor from one too many whiskeys-with-a-beer if I had someone closer to my age to pretend this kind of behavior was normal… a sibling, like everyone else seemed to have. Even a cousin who lived nearby would have done the trick. I wanted to be what I thought was American. I didn't know exactly what that was, but I knew that Americans didn't live like we did. Americans had more than one kid. Americans went out to eat in restaurants. Americans went to movies together, as families.

I wasn't interested in what had been good about my life and my parents in that year leading up to my wedding. My father had passed away from colon cancer the year before I met Hal. My mother and I weren't hurting for money as a result. I didn't give a fig about any of the sacrifices I'm sure my parents made in order for me to be the spoiled little princess I was then.

Ugh. I'm embarrassed to even say that, but it's true. And in that year before my wedding, I wanted to be part of what I thought was the "real" America, to stop being an outsider everywhere I went.

My fiancé's family was, in my mind, the perfect antidote.

To be married in the Catholic Church, one needs a baptismal certificate. This verified that yes, you were, to use the cliché, a card-carrying member of the Catholic Church. Your soul may be in peril from one of the many sins you committed during your time on Earth, but you were in the Protected Club because a priest had sprinkled holy water over your forehead when you were a baby.

There were pictures in a box in my mother's bedroom of my parents taking turns holding me on my baptism. I wore a white gown and bonnet, both of which were ill-fitting and probably borrowed at the last minute. My godparents, a taller set of Hungarians, also smiled and held my rather bewildered face up to the camera. The date on the back of one picture was December, 1962. I was a little over a year old. It certainly looked as though I'd been baptized according to the rites of Mother Church, but I needed a piece of paper that proved it before the Hungarian priest at the Hungarian Catholic Church would say a wedding mass for Hal and me.

I needed that paper to cleave unto a new, bigger, and, in my mind, better family.

Hal's family was a little disappointed at first that we weren't going to marry in the parish they called home. His mother, and her mother before her, had grown up in the same area of town. Hal's uncles were beloved first responders in that community. He had eleven first cousins, most of whom lived within a few miles of the area where they'd almost all grown up. Hal's grandmother met me for the first time in the matriarchal castle she'd owned for decades, a tidy little house behind a seawall with an expansive, gorgeous view of one of the Great Lakes. That picture window on the lake framed a living room featuring aqua carpet, pink furniture, and Grecian statues. And lots of pictures of family on the walls.

I wanted to get married in the Hungarian church on the other side of town. I didn't know many people in the parish, though some knew my mother. I'd moved her into a little 1930s house up the street from it not long after my father had passed. But my people, Hungarians, were the heart of the church and the reason for its existence. I was a Hungarian, albeit a reluctant one. I was the bride, and the wedding should be in my home parish, at least that's how I saw it.

But Father V, the kindly, if rather stern, pastor, said I needed a baptism certificate in order to make things happen.

My fiancé, of course, was able to pull his right out of the meticulously maintained baby book his mother started for him when he was a few days old. My mother knew nothing about any certificate, or how one obtained such a thing.

"Just call the priest at the church where they did your baptism," Father V explained in Hungarian. "They'll send it to you, and we'll be in business."

Annoyed at the need to do this at all, I rang up St. Dominica the Catholic church in the little Indiana town I called home. A fellow who sounded about twelve answered. I thought maybe it was the parish secretary's kid filling in or something.

"I'd like to speak with someone about getting a copy of my baptismal certificate," I said. I hoped I sounded cheery, although this guy seriously had enough cheeriness for both of us.

"I can help you with that," the twelve-year-old who subsequently identified himself as Father Name-Escapes-Me, the parochial vicar (second-in-command) of the parish. I gave him the particulars: name, parents' names, approximate date of baptism, and so forth. Of course, I could only give an approximate *month* of baptism since my mother didn't remember the exact date… or that it was even in December, or that it occurred, allegedly, in 1962. When I'd asked her about it, she'd gone off on a tangent about an argument she had with my godmother the morning of the baptism over whether or not she fed me properly.

My mother, like my father (whom everyone knew as Shorty), had fled from war-ravaged Hungary following a gaggle of friends to American shores in 1950. Violet was a sweet soul in many ways, but a terribly inexperienced mother and (excuse the seeming disrespect) not the sharpest tool in the shed. Her own parents had been teens when she was born. She'd been shuttled among disinterested relatives until, at last, she was dispatched to Catholic boarding school. She managed to finish before the war started.

Violet had no family role models. She'd never cared for an infant or small child. She didn't realize, for example, that she needed to furnish the clothing newborn me would be wearing home from the hospital. Her mothering—loving but inept—sort of just coasted along in the same vein over the ensuing years.

She tried. She failed a lot of times. But I knew she loved me.

* * *

"I found it," Father Name-Escapes-Me said with some triumph in his voice. "It was filed a little differently."

I looked at my watch. It had taken him more than a few minutes to find the damn thing. I just wanted to give him my address and get going on some other tasks, like making the final selection of meals to be served at the reception. I also didn't want my bosses catching me making these phone calls on the clock.

"The adopted daughter of Joseph and Violet Szabo, right?"

I thought I had heard wrong.

"Say that again, please?" I asked.

"The adopted daughter of…"

I stopped listening after I heard the word adopted.

What in holy hell was THIS?

I couldn't explain the sudden buzzing in my ears nor the sick feeling at the pit of my stomach. I remember telling myself to breathe, because I feared I wouldn't if I didn't make myself.

This man, this twelve-year-old-sounding man-boy, was essentially telling me my parents were not my parents.

I was adopted.

I was an adoptee.

The various groups of words raced through my mind, one string after another.

I was adopted.

ADOPTED.

In twenty-four years, not one person in my life had slipped about this secret.

To say I was stunned is probably an understatement.

What I don't remember is finishing the conversation, but I must have done so on autopilot, because the certificate came a few days later in the mail. Good to know I could still state my address accurately when my brain had melted into an unfeeling glob in my skull. Sure enough, that was my name on the certificate, right there with my parents' names—well, the names of the people I believed were my parents for twenty-four years—and a December, 1962 date on it, signed by the priest I'd known as a kid.

Twenty-four years. That kept coming back to me. Everyone around me...my parents, my parents' friends, the one or two relatives who occasionally floated in and out of our lives from Montreal or New Jersey... my godparents...my neighbors... everyone who had ever come in contact with me, throughout my *entire life,* had kept that secret.

Everyone.

I felt like the stupidest person in the world because me, Miss Big Brain, had never picked up on this possibility myself.

In my defense, I never had any significant reason to question my parentage. My parents were short; I was short. My mother had brown eyes; I had brown eyes. My father was pretty smart for a guy who had only finished junior high before his mother dropped dead next to him of a heart attack, and World War II came crashing down on him. I was smart, almost always the smartest kid in my class, so I figured that came from him. No, there wasn't a strong, oh-that's-definitely-their-kid resemblance between me and either of my parents, but I knew other people like that. A kid named Christine in one of my elementary school classes looked just like her grandmother, and I knew this because her grandmother had picked her up from school one day and I saw her and the long, pointed jaw she shared with Christine.

I only remember asking my father once, as he worked trimming a piece of wood in his garage workshop on a cool fall evening, if I was adopted. I was probably around nine.

I asked because I discovered earlier in the day that my friend Babette was adopted. My friend Lori asked her if she knew who her "real" parents were. Babette got all teary. No, strike that. She dissolved in a puddle of tears.

"My parents *are* my real parents," she replied amidst a flurry of sniffles and nose-wiping. Lori and I got in trouble from our teacher, Mrs. Bell, for making Babette cry and were told, in no uncertain terms, to mind our own business.

My father paused before answering me, something that didn't make me curious at the time. I asked him in English because I didn't know how to say "adopted" in Hungarian. Sometimes he had to think of the right English words to say, so a little waiting time before any of his responses was never a big deal.

"Would it make any difference if you were?" he asked, after a wait that seemed longer than usual.

"No, I guess not," I replied, genuinely feeling that it wouldn't. I felt kind of stupid for asking.

"So why would you even ask that question?"

Excellent deflection, Daddy. It put me off the scent of that possibility for years.

It was a given for my parents and me that we were a unit of three, a unit who lived in the here and now because there wasn't any place else to be. We were a family decimated by war and long distances. The only history we had lived inside my parents. That history was blotted and cracked by bombs and refugee camps and never knowing who to trust. It stayed locked away except for a few dribbles here and there when I was persistent in asking questions.

We had no scrapbooks or photo albums we could use to compare noses and eyebrows, no "family home" where pictures hung on the wall for generations to study. There was no grandmother to sit me on her lap and gush about how much I looked like her sister Margit. My parents didn't even have a photo of themselves on their wedding day. My mother told me when I was an adult that she had borrowed a gray suit to wear from a Romanian woman who'd borrowed it from a Bulgarian woman. ("It was a nice suit, even if it belonged to a Bulgarian. They're not known for their fashion sense," my mother sniffed when I asked her about her courthouse wedding.)

My parents fled famine, disease, violence, and the ruined rubble of their childhood neighborhoods in cold, hard, fear. Each had come separately with one suitcase to their names, passing through Ellis Island and by the Statue of Liberty on their way into the heartland of America. They had no place left to belong to except their new home— a strange and different place where they never could quite fit in. They met at a Hungarian church picnic in Detroit, given for single, youngish "new Americans" to meet others like themselves. They ended up, for better or for worse, belonging to each other. They left behind parents, siblings, cousins, lifelong friends… some of them alive, some of them not. They would never see most of those who managed to live through the war again.

All I felt, looking at that certificate, was that they belonged to each other, but I didn't belong to them.

And if I didn't belong to them… who did I belong to?

THE GIRL WITH OLIVE SKIN

1992

*H*ey, Anna. This is your researcher from Adoption Research Associates. If you have a few minutes, I have some information for you."

"Wait, let me close my office door. I didn't think I'd hear from you this quickly."

"You paid top dollar, you're getting top dollar services."

"I appreciate that. I just didn't know this would be... like this."

"You were lucky. You got me some great leads and made it a lot easier for me. Or did a private investigator get it for you?"

"I did hire a couple of other private investigators to find my birthparents over the last few years. Only one got me anything that could really help. I got a baptismal certificate from a Catholic church in Indianapolis. A priest from some parish near Indianapolis General had baptized me under my birthname. So I did at least learn I was born in Indianapolis. This same outfit, however, spent weeks trying to run down the name 'Pater Ignoto' to find my birthfather..."

(Laughter) "Father Unknown" in Catholic speak. You were lucky you got the information you did from the county courthouse. You got your birthmother's name and your first legal name—that's a real coup. Do you mind sharing how you got it? I know you're at work and everything, but I don't get clients who are such good detectives on their own very often."

"I don't know... it wasn't a lie, exactly, but it was on the shady side."

"Do tell. I love intrigue. And it might be useful to some of our other clients down the road."

"I sent a letter to the County, to the Clerk of Courts. My parents were living there when I was a baby, so I assumed they'd have the paperwork. I told them my adoptive father had passed away—which was true—but that I needed some proof of my adoption for the probate court in Ohio because that's where I live now. I was lucky I was in a different state and maybe they didn't know how those courts operate or something. The clerk sent me the court docket for the day of my adoption, which listed my birthmother's name. She also sent me the court order making the adoption final, which did not have my birthmother's name in it. It had the birthname she gave me, though."

"I don't want to sound like a snob, but sometimes you can really get things over on small town bureaucrats. That clerk didn't need to send you that court docket. Good to know—worked in Indiana, might work in some of those other Midwest states, too."

"Well, I looked at it as maybe someone felt sorry for me. I don't know, maybe that clerk was a birthmother or something... no, I told her it was for probate, so she wouldn't have made that kind of connection. Maybe she did and I'm not half as clever as I think I am...well, anyway...I appreciate any information you can give me. I found out by accident about six years ago that I was adopted. It took me a while to even decide to do this whole search thing."

By accident? Wow. I don't hear that a lot. Someone usually runs their mouth and gives the secret away. And you didn't find out until you were an adult? Amazing. Did you start looking right away?"

"Nope. I put it on the back burner, to be honest. I got married, I had a couple of babies... I was busy making Life happen, I guess. For a while I was mad that everyone knew this but me. Then I got angry at my birthparents for dumping me. I felt like finding them only to tell them good riddance."

"Yeah, some people feel like that. I don't get too many of those, but honestly, I do remember someone who wanted to do just that. But you changed your mind, obviously."

"When I had my own daughter a couple years ago, I realized that on my birthday, somewhere, someone had a daughter that was me. It's weird, but I didn't feel any need to search when I had my son. It was my daughter who made me want to know."

"You got in with a good adoptee search group at least. Elaine runs a tight ship there. I actually know her in person, one of the few people in the network who knows my real name."

"I suppose you have to be pretty tight-lipped about your work."

"That's an understatement. It's just safer, legally, the less you or anyone else

knows about how we get information. We have to be really careful in Indiana. They have the adoption registry—"

"Yes, I know about that. What a joke. It only lets grown adults have information about themselves if their adoptive parents and birthmother all sign papers saying it's okay. Only they conveniently neglect to let the public know it's available. Sorry, but they really pissed me off with their attitude when I contacted them."

"Indiana is in the Dark Ages in the adoption world."

"When I confronted my adoptive mother about being adopted, she said, 'They told us never to tell you.' I'll tell you what, that really frosted me, too. I love my adoptive parents, but they weren't very savvy about how things work in life. My mom didn't even speak English. I don't think they knew any better and did what they were told."

"That's what they used to tell everyone: never tell them they're adopted. Not even medical history, which is fricking unbelievable, if you ask me. Did your adoptive mother know any information she could give you? Or was she mad that you were searching? Wait, did she even know you were searching?"

"Not at first, but I eventually told her. She wasn't happy. She made some remark about how if my birth parents would have wanted me, they'd have kept me. I don't think she meant it to hurt me, but it did. So I didn't say anything more to her about it for a while. She didn't know anything anyway."

"That must have been rough."

"It is what it is."

"Yeah."

"You still there, Anna?"

"Yeah, sorry."

"Take a minute. This is heavy stuff. I can wait."

"No, you've got things to do and so do I. Anyway, the person who told me the most was my neighbor, who was the wife of the attorney who handled the adoption."

"What? That's bizarre. What did she tell you?"

"She said my birthmother was from the Philippines and was tiny with long, dark hair. Said she got pregnant here while she was in college as an exchange student or something and my birthfather abandoned her."

"Interesting story, but not completely correct according to the info I found. I assume Elaine and the group has talked to you about searching and the odds of a successful reunion, right? I always like to touch on that even though it's really none of my business. I just hate to think of people coming all this way and then being super hurt."

"Elaine said most people who find their birth parents end up rejected by them."

"Okay, so you know that. I always try to make sure my clients are prepared at least somewhat for what might happen once they get their information."

"You have enough for me to be able to actually find my birthmother?"

"I think so, yes."

Hello, are you there? You kind of gasped. Are you okay? Are you crying?"

"I'm okay. That was just a little... unexpected. It's hard to believe I might find this... person... Sorry."

"Happens a lot. I know this information is life-changing for people. I've had people really freak out on me. Elaine and the others will help you figure out how to best make contact, if that's what you decide. Are you ready to take down some information?"

"I'm ready. Go ahead."

"Do you have olive skin?"

"Um... as a matter of fact, I do."

"Logical. Mom is not from the Philippines. Mom is from Puerto Rico."

"I'm Puerto Rican?"

"I don't have any information on Dad to know if you're a full-blooded Puerto Rican, but Mom is definitely that."

"I grew up with Hungarian parents. I speak Hungarian. I know where Puerto Rico is, but that's about it."

"You'll have some homework, then, after we hang up. I've been there on vacation. Pretty island. I don't know a lick of Spanish though, so I was lost if we went outside San Juan."

"I don't know any Spanish either, except the textbook stuff I learned in college. Do you think she speaks English?"

"I have no idea. She has several American credit cards, though. She lives in Puerto Rico, and it looks like she's married. Her husband is a plant manager for a big company there. The best address I could get is P.O. Box 114, Humacao. That appears to be a current address."

"Well, she was a college student in Indiana—that's what my neighbor, the attorney's wife, said. So she must know English."

"I don't have any solid information on that. But I can confirm you were born in Indianapolis."

"Do you happen to know why my birth certificate doesn't say that? Do you have my real birth certificate, by chance?"

"They create new 'official' birth certificates for adoptees in lots of states. Indiana does that, too. I don't have a copy of your original birth certificate available. I do, however, have a phone number for your mom if you want that."

"Definitely. I feel nauseated thinking about calling it, but I want the number. And do you have any pictures of her?"

"I got a look at her driver's license. Nice looking lady. Her hair is short in the picture, by the way. But I don't have any other pictures."

"Can you get me that picture?"

"Not without getting arrested. I like helping clients, but not that much."

"Okay, forget I asked that. That's everything you have?"

"That should be enough for you to track her down. Like I said, all that information is current to the best of my knowledge."

"Can I call you back if I think of any other questions?"

"Once I hang up with you, I'll be destroying this information. It's a one-shot deal. We don't want to jeopardize any of our contacts."

"Or get into legal trouble."

"That, too."

"I really appreciate this information. You don't know how much. Can I ask you, before you go, why you do this?"

"I make really good money doing it."

"You don't have an adoption connection yourself?"

"No, I don't. Years ago I met someone who was involved in this kind of investigative searching, and I just kind of fell into it. Like I said, the money is

good."

"People are desperate, I guess. I suppose I am, too. It's been nagging at me for so long. I want to know who I am and who my people are."

"Understandable. I wish you luck and hope you find what you're looking for."

"Thanks again... I'm sorry, I didn't catch your name."

"As far as you're concerned, I don't have one. Safer that way. So good luck. Nice talking with you."

BECAUSE THEY'RE NOT ME

1992

I learned a lot about the "New Me," the Puerto Rican me, in the weeks immediately following the call from my adoption researcher. What I learned, however, wasn't what I was expecting.

After I spoke with Mysterious Agent X, or MAX, as I had come to refer to him in my head, I carried around the nuggets of information he'd given me as if they were precious stones. I hadn't decided what, if anything, I was going to do with the stolen bits and pieces of her life that I'd raided my inheritance to buy.

January, 1992 turned into February, 1992. February creeped toward March.

"When are you going to call her?"

I must have gotten that question a dozen times a day from my extended family-by-marriage. My mother-in-law—excited and happy for me—had gone through her Rolodex, so to speak, calling most everyone she knew and speculating endlessly with them about what I might discover if I'd just get brave enough to pick up the phone. Supportive, yes. They all were. But more impatient than anything. And curious, wanting to see the new animal on display in the family zoo.

"I suppose you'll learn to speak Spanish now," one friend remarked upon hearing the news. "That'll take you what, a day to learn with your brains?"

"You just have to sound like you're angry whenever you talk. That'll do it," another relative chimed in. "And talk super fast."

Another joked at a family dinner that when it was my turn to host the meal, the entrée of choice had to be tacos. Tacos.

My education about the identity I was trying on for size had begun.

I hadn't thought much about the fact that I was now, by blood, a person of Hispanic heritage. Well, I had always been—I just hadn't known it. And since I hadn't known it, I wasn't exactly egalitarian in my past references to my fellow Hispanics in my "previous life."

"All this time we've joked about the "Ezzes" around here and come to find out you're an Ez, too!"

A dear friend said this to me on a rainy afternoon when I told her of my chat with MAX. "Ez"—SanchEZ, PerEZ, ValdEZ, etc. How many times had I said that with her? No, how many times had I *laughed* when I said that right along with her?

How many times had I said nothing when I heard words like "spic" and "wetback" and "beaner"?

A "joke" that had been popular in my small-town high school: What's the best kind of can to shoot? Mexi-CANS, Puerto Ri-CANS, and Domini-CANS.

I hadn't objected to it, no matter how many times I heard it, even though I knew, as a child of "foreigners" myself, the "joke" was cruel and hurtful.

Because those "cans" were not me. Being an Ameri-CAN was not the same.

I was afraid to call my Puerto Rican birthmother for a lot of reasons. But one of them was because I was ashamed of myself, and of so many people I loved. I couldn't bring myself to condemn them, or me. I knew these beliefs were common where I grew up, and that most people who held them were not horrible and unfeeling. I made a lot of excuses for myself, and for them.

In my neck of the woods, both growing up and after I moved to the city, those of Hispanic descent were mostly Mexicans. They picked fruits and vegetables in the fields, or they worked in the non-union factories. I'd hear snippets of their music if "a carload of them" pulled up next to me. It was loud, horns blaring, with the same beat pounding throughout a song. I saw them kneeling next to me at Mass on Sundays, their children scrubbed clean and lined up like dolls next to them. Mexican food was good, if you liked tacos, enchiladas, and margaritas. I could drop into the local Mexican restaurant, hoist a few 'ritas with some chips and salsa, and go home to my world without a second thought. Some Mexicans—and they were all Mexicans, because the idea that they could be Hondurans, Guatemalans, Panamanians, or even Puerto Ricans didn't come to mind—were the servers who brought me my steaming fajitas and refilled my drinks.

But did I really see them?

No.

Because they were not me.

I had grown up in a world that found my Hungarian roots interesting and out-of-the-ordinary. I heard about it all the time. It was a point of pride with me.

"I just love to hear you speak with your mom. That language sounds like nothing I've ever heard before."

"Your dad Shorty was a real example of the American dream. He came here from Hungary with nothing, and he built himself a nice house on a farm and made a good life for you."

I tested the waters with a few people in the weeks after "the call"— co-workers, acquaintances, extended family—and mentioned that my heritage now included Puerto Rican.

"Is that right?"

"Well, that's certainly different, isn't it?"

"Where is that, exactly?"

"I went there on a cruise once. Nice place, but awfully crowded."

"Bet you weren't expecting that."

I didn't recall getting those raised eyebrows, those changes in vocal tone, those vague responses, when I mentioned my parents were from Hungary. This wasn't everybody, mind you, but there were enough reactions like that to make me stop and think.

And after my biological roots became more public knowledge, the saddest remark I heard came from yet another friend, also well-meaning, also American like me.

"Well, it's good you ended up being adopted like you were. Who knows what kind of crappy life you would have had being Mexican."

Not Mexican. Puerto Rican. *Puerto Rican.*

And how do you know it would have been "crappy"?

I had no idea what my life would have been like had I not been given up for adoption. But in those weeks that followed my call from MAX, I sure thought about it a lot. And I felt a hell of a lot of guilt for the way I had viewed and talked about Spanish people—now, at least on paper, MY people.

* * *

Late April, 1992. I still didn't make the call.

I looked at the phone number probably fifty times a day.

I looked at her name. Iluminada Galvez Perez. Melodic, flowing, extraordinary. Surely belonging to a beautiful young woman with long dark hair and puppy-dog eyes who could glide across a room like a dancer, whose laugh was a sweet little tinkle of a bell.

Not like Violet. Violet was short with perpetually unruly hair, always a beat behind everyone in movement and thought, seeing judgement and rejection where there wasn't any. Violet didn't glide. She snuck through life, her defense shields always up, relying on others to chart her course. She was not Iluminada.

I imagined Iluminada signing that mellifluous name on the papers that gave me away. I imagined her crying, no, sobbing, as she did it. Who were these monsters in Indiana who were taking her baby? Had she seen me? Had she held me?

On darker days, I imagined her signing with a cavalier toss of that long black hair I always imagined she really had, dry-eyed, because she would no longer have to deal with her unfortunate mistake. I'd been born on a cool, but not cold, day. She had to at least put a light coat on as she strode out of the hospital in late November, 1961, probably to get on a plane that would whisk her back home to her sunny island, without the "problem" of me to weigh her down. She could glide again, free and unencumbered.

Which had it been? Did she want me or not?

I imagined her face. Was it like mine? Was it like my father's? Because I had to have a birthfather, too, not just a birthmother. I hated those terms, birthmother and birthfather. They sounded cold. But I had a father and mother, Shorty and Violet. I had parents who loved me. I couldn't call those other people my parents, even though technically, they were.

If they'd have truly loved me, they'd never have given me away.

But maybe they had to. Maybe theirs had been a dramatic, doomed romance destined to crash and burn, and I was the casualty. Maybe my birthfather had gone out for cigarettes and never came back, and my birthmother had no choice. Maybe they'd wanted to marry, but the universe conspired against them and they had to give each other up as well as me.

Two mothers, two fathers. I belonged to both, yet neither. Most of the time, it gave me a headache to think about it all. Headaches and a lot of tears.

So instead, I devoured information about Puerto Rico.

Three million people, more or less, all of whom were American citizens who could come back and forth from the island as they chose. People descended from the Taíno tribe of native Americans; their ancestors—and perhaps mine—had greeted Columbus and the juggernaut of European settlers who came after him. Most Taíno eventually paid for that visit with their lives, whether through disease, slavery, murder, or all three. A lot of those European settlers came from the Canary Islands and southern Spain. My birthmother's family names had likely come with these settlers, ages ago, with names ending in -ez. Iluminada Galvez Perez. The language of Spain had stayed, the language she surely had grown up speaking.

Apparently, a lot of single young men came to Puerto Rico in the years immediately after its discovery by Europeans, with the idea of serving God and getting rich in the process. Columbus had christened the island Puerto Rico, or "rich port" in Spanish. But the Taíno to whom it belonged called it *Borikén*. In their language, it meant "Land of the Valiant and Noble Lord," the Great Creator. The young men with grand ambitions helped the new "lords" make the island theirs. Along the way, since the native population had died and/or intermarried, Africans were "imported" to work the plantations that sprung up across the island.

I could not only be Spanish and Native American... I could be African, too. I thought that was kind of cool, to be honest. But I knew that in some corners of my world, that wasn't going to go over well if it was true.

Then I read that Italians, Germans, Irish, and even Jews were part of later waves of immigration to the island.

I could be anything.

But I probably wasn't Hungarian. At least not by blood.

"Your soul is Hungarian and always will be," said a dear friend from college, Antal, whose parents were also from Hungary. He'd listened to the endless whining and complaining I'd done over the years since I'd first found out I was adopted, raging at why information about me had to be kept secret. He'd heard me growl about not even being able to obtain medical information about these blood relatives lurking out somewhere in the shadows.

He always had the right words at the right time.

"You know there are lots of Hungarians who are actually Romanians or Slavs. Their ancestors ended up in Hungarian territory because of all the wars. There are tons of people who love Hungary and consider themselves Hungarian, even if their blood technically isn't. That's you. We're not going to kick you out of the club."

We're not going to kick you out of the club. You, the real Hungarians, will let me stay on.

He didn't mean it that way. He was, and remains, a caring, gentle soul. He wasn't trying to make me feel inferior. He'd been trying to console me, to reassure me I was still who I had always been.

I took his words that way because inside me, I didn't know who I was anymore.

Puerto Ricans were not me. I'd never been anywhere close to a Caribbean island in my life.

Mexicans, the default Hispanic heritage in my area of the American Midwest, were not me.

Hungarians were now, somehow, not me, either.

I was American, yes. But Americans bragged about being Irish or Italian or German or Swedish, too. They knew, or at least acted like they knew, their people and felt like they belonged to them.

I was me, all by myself. As I had throughout my entire life, for

reasons I still can't explain, I wanted to belong *somewhere.*
And still I belonged, in those weeks, to no one.

TELL HER I LOVE HER

1992

When I look back on it, the place was a bit seedy. Like 1972-low-budget-film seedy. Rattling, gasping air conditioner. Orange curtains with loud, jarring geometric patterns. Lime green walls. A miniscule bathroom and a shower that spit lukewarm water. The whole room needed a good scrubbing, or maybe bleaching, or maybe just gutting to start over again. Thankfully, I'd seen no signs that it needed fumigating, too.

I was in Tampa, Florida, in a tired-looking hotel with an interstate shoe-horned in next to it. We'd been told it was one of the top hotels for tourists visiting Busch Gardens, the amusement park a few blocks up the road.

These tourists didn't seem to have very high standards in my mind.

But in this silly-looking, outdated room, I waited to hear what my birthmother thought of me.

* * *

I'd eventually taken that information MAX gave me and handed it over to a friend, Andy, who was in corporate security, but had a background in investigative work. By his own admission, he had no experience in the shadowy world of adoption research. I tried to hire Andy to get to the finish line, so to speak—to check it all out, —make sure it was legit. There was the possibility that MAX made all that stuff up, or was at least partially wrong about some or all of the facts. I felt good that I stalled about making the call, actually, because I convinced myself that I didn't want to intrude on a perfectly innocent woman's life and make trouble for her where there wasn't any. What if I called the wrong woman? What if I made her husband and family suspicious of her past?

Ay, an anxious mind makes up a lot of reasons to put things off.

Anyway, he said I'd be better off hiring specialists in that area and was reluctant to help me, albeit because he "didn't want to take my money and disappoint me."

"Why haven't you called your birth mom already?"

Hal and I, along with our small children, were kicking back for an evening at Andy's house in April, 1992. His wife, Sherri, worked with me—although not for much longer, since I had put in my two-week notice at the physicians' practice where we were both employed. That was how the friendship had begun.

"I don't know," I said. "I can't. I'm too afraid."

"Andy, what if her mother doesn't even speak English?" Sherri asked.

"That'd be a problem," Hal said.

"Why don't *you* call her?" Sherri said to Hal.

"I think she should do it. It would be weird coming from me," Hal said.

"Why don't you call her in the capacity of a private investigator or something else official like that?" I asked Andy.

He furrowed his brow.

"I'll think about it," he said. "But seriously, I think it should come from you, too."

"I can't do it," I said.

The conversation turned to other things, although I noticed Andy kept glancing at me with a tinge of sadness in his eyes. He looked uncomfortable, like he was trying to get up the courage to say something but lost it at the last minute. Hal's and my decision to move to Florida dominated the evening's chatter, but Andy never quite left the topic of my adoption search and how it was now lying in the dust of my fear.

"You're going house-hunting in Florida this weekend?" Sherri asked between mouthfuls of hot dogs and hamburgers from Andy's grill.

"I'm meeting with a company in Tampa to finalize the terms of the job they offered me," Hal said. "We figured we'd kill two birds with one stone and do some quick house-shopping, too."

"I suppose that's a good idea, since you have the house auction up here scheduled already," Andy said. "This is kind of moving quickly, though, isn't it?"

Andy looked at me again. I looked away.

"Oh, it's all a done deal," Hal replied with his usual confidence, bouncing our toddler daughter on his knee. "We'll find something. Houses are a lot cheaper down there than they are here. We'll get rid of the house up here and be down there by the end of May."

Hal. Always self-assured. Always confident that what *he* wanted was what was best for everyone and would happen without so much as a hitch. I had some reservations about moving so far away from the family I'd wanted so badly to join. But that family had splintered and fractured. My in-laws were no longer together. Some family members were in therapy. Others no longer spoke to one another. It was a depressing situation, and Hal didn't like "depressing" anything.

"We want to live somewhere our children won't hate," Hal added. "That way they won't grow up and move away from us."

"What about your mom?" Sherri asked, meaning Violet.

"She's staying here for now. She has the apartment in the same building as Eleanor…"

"Eleanor?" Sherri interrupted me to ask.

"Hal's grandmother," I said. "Mama likes this setup, because Eleanor takes her everywhere. For now, until we figure things out down there, she stays here."

"Where are you staying this weekend?" Andy asked as we packed up toys and diaper bags and plates of leftovers, ready to head home.

"A hotel—a Best Western, I think—on Busch Boulevard," I said. "The one closest to Busch Gardens."

"Call us when you get there to let us know you made it okay," Andy replied.

That was odd. We weren't that close of friends, and it wasn't like we were flying into some dangerous airport on the other side of the world. We were leaving Thursday morning and returning Sunday. We weren't even taking the kids.

But I agreed to call.

* * *

"Don't be mad at me," Andy said.

That was suspicious.

I had called when we made it to the hotel as he'd asked. I'd called him, not Sherri, because I knew she wouldn't easily be able to take a call at work since she was constantly seeing patients. He'd asked for our room number. He called back just as Hal and I were returning to the room from dinner.

"I asked my mom to call your birthmother."

"What? Are you kidding me? After all that, saying you thought it would be weird for anybody else but me to call her, you asked your mom to do it? And why your mom? Your mom doesn't even know me!"

"Mom speaks Spanish," Andy said. "Remember... you guys were wondering how much English your birthmom speaks? Well, I figured the call would be best coming from someone who was around her age and spoke Spanish. If her husband answered, then she was going to pretend to be an old friend from the States."

"She TALKED TO HER?"

I was shouting. Hal pestered me to let him in on what was going on. The room spun.

I handed the phone to Hal and ran into the bathroom.

Hal eventually came to see me. I used the closed toilet as a seat. I shook badly.

"Marilisa talked to your birthmother," he said. He sat on the edge of the bathtub and took my hand.

"Marilisa?" I asked.

"Andy's mom. She's going to call us here, in about an hour, to tell us what your birthmother said."

"It's not good, is it?" I said.

Hal wiped away a few tears from my cheeks.

"Andy didn't go into much detail. He said he'd rather have his mom say it in her own words. Honestly, I didn't get a sense from Andy about how it went. He was very... careful."

It wasn't even an hour before the phone rang. I asked Hal to take the call and speak with Marilisa. I felt like I was going to throw up. I closed the bathroom door so I wouldn't hear what was being said. I couldn't. All this searching, all this anguish and money and wondering who she was and who I was… ending in a bathroom a thousand miles from the only home I had ever known.

She had rejected me. I felt it in my heart. The door had shut. I didn't know what Marilisa said to my husband, but I knew it wasn't what I wanted to hear. And no matter how much the adoption support group had tried to prepare me, I didn't realize it would hurt this badly to hear, even just in my imagination, the word "no."

* * *

Hal spent a long while on the phone with Marilisa. I opened the bathroom door just as he was placing the phone handset back on its cradle. We sat on the bed, and he told me the story of the phone call.

Marilisa had called Iluminada in the early evening, a little after 5 p.m. in Puerto Rico. Marilisa was in Texas, behind an hour. Iluminada might be walking in from work around then. There was no way to know for certain that the Iluminada Marilisa was calling was indeed my birthmother. There was no way to know what, if anything, Iluminada's husband knew about the situation. So Marilisa didn't want to take any chances. She had never made a phone call like this. But she knew she'd likely only have a short window in which to give—or get—information.

Iluminada gasped and fell silent at hearing Marilisa's opening words.

"My name is Marilisa, and I think you may know something about my son's friend, a woman who was born in Indianapolis on November 14, 1961."

Iluminada began crying.

"My son is a private investigator, and he thinks his friend is your daughter. Is he right?" Marilisa asked. She'd almost whispered the words, as if softening them would somehow make a difference in how the woman on the other end of the line would accept them.

Iluminada told Marilisa that she did, indeed, have a daughter who was born on that day. A daughter she had to give away. A daughter no one knew about.

"I was a school teacher for most of my life. Every time I wrote that date on my blackboard, I would start to cry, and I could never tell the children why I was sad," Iluminada said. "I have wondered every day of my life since then how she is and if she is still alive, if she is happy, if she knows anything about me."

Marilisa told her that her daughter was grown and happy, living in Ohio, married with two children, and that she would soon be moving to Florida.

Marilisa told Iluminada that her daughter would like to get to know her.

Iluminada began to sob.

"Tell my daughter I love her. Tell her I love her. But I can't face her. I can't let my family know about this. I will always love her. But I cannot speak to her or see her."

"So you want me to tell her to never contact you again?" Marilisa asked.

"Tell her I love her. I love her with all my heart. But she cannot contact me again. Tell her I'm sorry and will never forgive myself for not being her mother like I should have been."

I wiped away a few stray tears. I had been right. All of a sudden, I felt a strange calm inside. There was no more wondering. For reasons I thought I would never know, my birthmother didn't raise me. She signed papers handing my fate over to the state of Indiana, perhaps with hope they would see to it that her child was looked after. She went home to Puerto Rico without me.

But Iluminada, my mother...my first mother... loved me.

* * *

By noon the next morning, Hal had signed a contract for a new job. By dinnertime, we put in an offer on the fourth house we'd seen. I had never done anything so, well, reckless, in my life. I was charmed by the palm trees everywhere, the warm, humid breeze wafting around us, the rows of pastel houses with manicured yards, the blue sky and sun blazing overhead. Florida was bedazzling on that day. It was going to be my new home. I would be moving far away from the farm a half-mile away from the road, the farm to which Shorty and Violet had brought me as a newborn so many years ago. It didn't escape me that my new home would be roughly halfway between my home in Indiana and my birthmother's home in Puerto Rico.

Two sets of parents. And now, two places to call home.

My heart was heavy through dinner.

"We knew this might end this way," Hal tried to reassure me. "She told Marilisa she loved you. At least you know that. Most of your adoptee friends didn't even get that."

That was true. Almost all of the adoptees in my group who had made contact with their birthparents had been turned away. In one case, the birthfather was receptive but the birthmother was not. In several other instances, the birthmother had already passed away, and with them went the identities of the birthfathers. Marilisa had not asked Iluminada about my birthfather, so I was destined to never know who he was. I wouldn't have thought to ask her that myself, truth be told. He may not have even known about me. The little paperwork I did have listed him as "Pater Ignoto" —father unknown.

I had given it my best shot and come up empty, like the others.

* * *

The message light blinked on the clunky room phone when we got back to the hotel in the evening, around 7:00. The message, the front desk clerk said, was from Marilisa.

"Maybe she forgot to tell us something important," Hal said. "Call her back."

There was no reason for me now to be shaking and nauseated about anything. I made the call.

"Listen," Marilisa said when I had her on the line. "I hope you don't mind that I did this, but I called your birthmother back."

Honestly, I felt both appreciative and annoyed. This woman—and I had gone to referring to Iluminada as 'this woman' in my head over the last twenty-four hours, already trying to put distance between us again—had already made it clear she didn't want anything to do with me. She loved me, yes, but not enough to make me a part of her life. I confess, my heart hardened a little bit from last night to this moment. I put the ball in Iluminada's court, and she sent it back and walked off. But Marilisa had already done so much for me with that one phone call. I couldn't imagine what else she might have had to discuss with Iluminada. I hoped the second call hadn't gotten Iluminada in trouble with her family.

"The tone of her voice didn't match her words in the first call," Marilisa explained. "She was saying she didn't want you to contact her. But I guess I just didn't believe her. It didn't sound right. So I called back and offered her one last chance to get your information."

My heart hammered in my chest.

"And?" was all I could ask.

"She began sobbing up a storm. She said she'd been praying all night that the lady who knew where her daughter was would call her again. She regretted telling me no, and she wants you to send her a letter and some pictures. She will answer you if you do that, but she wants to know how you feel about her first."

Every fellow guest in that shady hotel must have heard the shriek I let out.

Marilisa told me more. Panicked, Iluminada had originally said no one knew about me. In fact, her husband Raúl did know. He had wanted to find me, she said, and would have raised me as his own. But she'd been too afraid. The officials in Indiana treated her coldly and shamed her for having a baby "with no father," in their words. She wanted to try and forget, like they told her she would do.

But she never could.

Raúl and Iluminada had three sons together, but they never told them about me. Nor had they told any of the extended family.

Iluminada's father, my grandfather, was a staunch Catholic. He told Iluminada, point blank, that she could not "bring a child conceived in sin" into his home. No one would want to marry Iluminada with a "bastard" hanging around her neck. My birthfather was married to someone else, so there could be no assistance coming from him.

My birthfather. I had one.

I got lost in that thought for a moment, and ended up having to ask Marilisa to repeat what else Iluminada said.

Iluminada said her husband wasn't home because he worked at night, but Raúl told her to get up the courage to call that woman back. The girl was reaching out to them, he said. They had to open their arms to her.

Iluminada said she refused to take Marilisa's number and couldn't call.

So Iluminada prayed.

As I heard this, tears streaming, I had a quick, cynical moment. Iluminada had likely prayed and prayed when she was pregnant with me. If there had been an answer at all, if there was a "Dios" in the sky listening to her prayers, the answer had been to move on and get over it … the answer was no. I will not help you with this baby.

This time, "Dios" said yes.

ADALEE LIVES

1992

I Pulled a newspaper clipping out of my purse, sitting yet again in the same seedy hotel where I'd heard Marilisa tell me Iluminada loved me. The world had changed tremendously in the few weeks since that call.

Local woman to meet her mother for the first time on Mother's Day.

I don't remember now who contacted a local newspaper columnist, the kind who writes lots of feel-good stories, to tell him about me finding my birthmother. I know it wasn't me. It could have been Hal or one of his family members. Hal spoke to the columnist when he called since I wasn't home.

The whole city knew, if they'd read that column, that I was flying to Florida again to meet my birthmother. She was flying from Puerto Rico to meet me.

Violet told me to have a safe flight.

"You know you will always be my 'real' mother to me, right?"

Violet was stony-faced, perched on the forty-year-old couch in her apartment, the one that had been in every living room of hers I could remember. She wasn't convinced.

"That's what you say," she replied.

The last few weeks had been a roller coaster ride of epic proportions. I was no longer working, but packing boxes and juggling the care of two small children in preparation for our move south. The house was supposed to have sold at auction—our choice, because it was a faster way of selling than listing it with a realtor. But a rival auctioneer had placed a phony bidder at the auction, one who won the bidding but said, after all the other buyers had departed, that he didn't actually have the money to buy the place. No, that is not illegal, or at least it wasn't in Ohio in 1992. We were able to cobble together an alternative way to finance our new home and find a renter for the house we were leaving... but that, too, had taken a tremendous amount of energy and worry to make happen.

Our bank accounts were draining, too. Another flight to Florida, a special one sandwiched between the house-hunting one and the final one which would take us south for good, wasn't helping.

Violet's resentment wasn't helping, either. My anxiety at coordinating a cross-country move and meeting a person with such a tremendous impact on my life and identity wasn't helping, either. I lost a lot of sleep, more than what I naturally lost being the mother of two little kids.

But there we were in the Best Western again, this time in a room that had a view of the fountain in the central courtyard, waiting to see my birthmother for the first time. It was May 10, 1992.

A couple of weeks earlier, right after Marilisa made her calls, I'd gotten a few calls myself.

"I don't have the right words to tell you how happy I am that you found us," Iluminada said in nearly perfect English. "I hope I won't disappoint you."

Well, I now knew where my relentless streak of pessimism came from.

"You are like winning the lottery," her husband Raúl —now my stepfather, technically—asked her to tell me, since he spoke no English. "We just won our baby girl back. Nadi and I are very, very happy."

Nadi. They called her Nadi.

Three brothers called me, one after the other, a bit dazed from the news they had a sister, but warm and welcoming, eager to meet me. Raúl gave them the lottery story as he broke the news to each.

"I thought he was going to tell us they won all this money, and the family was rich now," the eldest of my three younger brothers, Aaron, told me. "But this kind of win is much better."

No hesitancy. No suspicion that I was a phony or a gold-digger or a scam artist. I confess I might have wondered that had the whole thing happened in reverse and the family contacted me out of the blue first.

Aaron and his family, a wife and two small children very close in age to mine, lived in a Florida city a few hours from Tampa. Iluminada was flying from Puerto Rico to his home, and he and his family were going to drive her to Tampa to meet me and Hal.

May 10, 1992.

I wore a black and white top with matching bottoms. I wanted to hide my chunkiness and deluded myself into thinking that would do the trick. I waited at the window of the hotel room overlooking the courtyard. It was the same hotel where my life had been changed a few weeks earlier, though a better room than the last time. I went outside the room to wait at the railing. I could hear the rush of the fountain below. People—travelers with suitcases, custodians mopping the floors, a delivery man with a cart of packages—they were all going about their normal days.

I was waiting to meet the woman who gave me life.

And a few minutes after I stepped out to the railing to wait, I saw a hand waving at me from the floor below.

My mother was here. After almost thirty-one years, my mother was here.

I ran down the stairs and crashed into her waiting arms, Hal close behind me. He, and my brother and his family, let us have our moment.

It was the longest, and one of the warmest, embraces I have ever felt in my life.

She dressed a lot like me with a matching set of top and bottom herself. Her hair was indeed short, a rich dark brown, just about the same shade as mine. She was a little shorter than I am. Her hands looked exactly like mine. Her eyes were brown, like mine.

She pulled away, finally, and clasped my shoulders, a look of wonder in those brown, teary eyes.

"You look just like your father!"

"Is that good?" I asked, not knowing what else to say.

"Oh, he was so handsome, and you're so beautiful. You look just like him."

A lot of the next few minutes was a whirlwind. My brother—I had THREE BROTHERS!—and his family were adorable. I didn't see much resemblance between him and me. I didn't care. He was my brother. His children were my niece and nephew. I had a sister-in-law who wasn't related to Hal.

99

"I have never seen Mami this happy," Aaron said to me in the midst of our embrace. "You are a gift she can hardly believe is real."

In that fleeting moment, with my mother's arms wrapped around me, I joined another tribe, the tribe that had been mine from the day I was born.

Giddy, heart beating like a drum, I looked into Nadi's eyes.

"May I call you Mami?"

Nadi began to cry.

"I never thought I would hear that word from my daughter," she replied. "I am your mother. What else would you call me?"

* * *

"I went to Indiana University to earn an extra teaching certificate to teach English as a second language," Nadi explained as we sat in the hotel room.

Hal, Aaron, and his family had gone off to the hotel restaurant after checking the family's bags in to their own room. So very kind, they all wanted my mother and me to have our time together, just the two of us.

"So you're a teacher?" I asked.

"I was one for thirty years. I retired last year."

She told me about my grandfather, her father, who wouldn't let her come home with me because I had been "conceived in sin." She also told me about my grandmother, who was "stuck with the same long, terrible name she had, Iluminada" but who had blue eyes and a kind heart. "No one else in the family had blue eyes," Nadi said.

My children did.

Nadi told me about marrying Raúl the year after I was born, and how he encouraged her to look for me and "get her back".

"He is a wonderful man. He loves you like his own already, and he can't wait to meet you."

Raúl had stayed behind in Puerto Rico because of his work. I learned later he wanted Nadi to have this moment in the sun for herself, to do this on her own without relying on him.

I relied on Hal for a lot of the various parts of this journey, just as she apparently had relied on Raúl to help her get through the roughest parts.

I had never met anyone who was so much like me.

I interrupted her story of Raúl and what a wonderful father he was to their three sons.

"What is my father's name?"

I was afraid of asking that question before I met her. I didn't know if he had attacked her, or he used her, or what kind of relationship they had. But when she said he was "so handsome," I thought it might be okay to ask.

"Your father is Lee Satterfield. He was so handsome, like I told you. He looked like Perry Mason."

Perry Mason, the debonair television lawyer from the 60s. I watched old episodes of that show with Violet a lot. We both thought the actor who played him, Raymond Burr, was handsome.

"He was always very serious like Perry Mason, too," Nadi said. "He was a scientist of some kind... I don't remember what he was studying, but he was in grad school at the university."

I had just gone from a first-generation college graduate to the child of two college-educated parents... a whole different kind of pride than what I felt since earning my degree in journalism. And my father was a scientist. I loved science.

The whole nature vs nurture thing... for me, nurture was going down in flames. I was nothing like my parents—wait, how was I going to refer to everyone now? I had a Mama and a Mami. I had a Daddy and a, well, Dad for lack of any other term. Not that I was even thinking about finding him at that moment. It was enough to know he had a name, and I had gotten at least one thing, my love of science, from him.

"He grew up in Indiana, so he was a... what is that word they call people born in Indiana?"

"Hoosier," I said, laughing.

"You and he are both Hoosiers," she replied, laughing as well.

Lee was married with three children, Nadi explained. Nadi had flown home after earning her certificate in May, 1961, pregnant with me but not yet showing. Her father told her to go back to Indiana and "deal with her problem," because that child wasn't coming to live with him.

Nadi ended up living in the basement of Lee's mother, my other grandmother, for a few months until there was room in an unwed mothers' home in Indianapolis. She tried to squeeze her rapidly expanding self behind the washing machine, she told me, hiding every time Lee's children came for a visit.

That secret was kept from his kids, but not his wife. His wife offered to take me in after I was born and raise me herself, as one of her own children. Lee and Nadi turned down that idea, she said.

So Nadi spent the last few weeks of her pregnancy in a home for unwed mothers, watching a lot of television and existing on bland, flavorless food.

I was born by C-section on a chilly afternoon in November. The doctor, she said, was very kind, and told her everything would be fine.

She tried to sneak down to see me, though they told her she was expressly forbidden from doing so. I was in what she called a "side nursery," away from public view, before beginning to cry.

"I figured this was the nursery where they put the babies who wouldn't be allowed to go home with their mothers."

I was in an incubator, weighing only a little over four pounds. She saw lots of wires attached to me. And I kept crying. No, screaming, she corrected herself.

"You were crying because you couldn't be with me, and I always felt like you were so angry because somehow you knew you would never be with your mother, that your mother was leaving you behind."

A nurse found her and took her back to her room.

She never saw me again until this day.

* * *

Among the rush and joy of these moments I will never forget, I received gifts from Nadi and the family.

One was an engraved plaque. A red, engraved rose graced the

bottom of it, with the date of our reunion beneath. The words on top were simple:

May the joy of this encounter show me the way to go on.

Nadi hadn't known if I would be angry with her in person, or if we would feel no spark or bond upon meeting. She chose the words that she was feeling. Later I would look at them and feel a little twinge of hurt in my heart. I didn't know what to say or feel, either. It was uncharted territory, one that came with no manuals or road maps. We loved each other, in a very specific way, from that first magical moment in which we met.

But we were not mother and daughter.

We were strangers who would have to build a relationship from scratch, as adults, with all the baggage we would both be bringing along.

The other gift was a small Puerto Rican flag to hang from the rearview mirror of my car.

"You can put this in your car now," Aaron said with obvious pride. "You're Puerto Rican."

I didn't speak Spanish. I had never been to the island. I'd never tasted any Puerto Rican food. Secretly, I still didn't like Spanish music. I had no idea of what that meant, to "be Puerto Rican."

But a few weeks later, sitting in the newish van Hal and I purchased after our move to Florida, I hung the flag on my mirror.

I was Nadi's daughter now.

I counted as a person of color. I counted as someone of Hispanic heritage.

But I was a lot of other things, too.

It was difficult to mix them into one big pot.

THE BIRTHDAY PARTY

1993

"I got you a party hat just in case."

Nadi and I stood at a table festooned with streamers on a warm, overcast day in a home in Puerto Rico.

Puerto Rico.

An island that, until eighteen months ago, rarely crossed my mind. It was an island that I now heard, over and over again, was "my home."

I, along with Hal and the children, was here to celebrate what Nadi called my "first" birthday... because it was the first one I would be spending with her. We both dismissed the fact that, technically, we had been together, however briefly, on the actual day I was born. That day had been Shorty and Violet's day, the day they could rejoice that the baby they had waited years for had arrived.

The festive table was peppered with confetti, multi-colored metallic balloons tethered to its legs and bouncing above it. A cake, thick with sugary frosting and huge fondant flowers, took the place of honor in the middle of the table. Nadi held what I would have called a birthday tiara rather than a hat, but it was for me, and she had chosen it. Clearly, I inherited my love of shiny, gaudy things from her.

I would be celebrating my birthday for the first time with Nadi, Raúl, one brother and sister-in-law, and a slew of relatives whom I'd never met, some of whom spoke little or no English. I was terribly excited, if a bit nervous.

The aunts, uncles, cousins, and in-laws coming were *my* relatives.

I was telling Nadi it had gotten confusing, sometimes, to some of my childhood friends as I explained my new, much more complex family configuration.

"I told an old friend I was going to visit my mother in Puerto Rico and meet a lot of my extended family," I said. "She got confused, of course, because she knew my Hungarian mama had passed away."

Nadi's eyes teared up in a brief flicker of pain that slipped away as quickly as it had come. She cut me off as I tried to tell the rest of that story.

"You just need to tell people you're not adopted anymore," Nadi said.

The cake on the table certainly conveyed that message.

"Welcome Home, Adalee," it said.

Adalee… the name she gave me.

She'd chosen Ada, she said, because it was short and easy to pronounce—not like her own name, which she disliked immensely. She added the "Lee" because that was my birthfather's name.

"All his other children had the middle name Lee, that's what he told me," Nadi said emphatically when she first told me how she'd chosen my name. "You were one of his children, and I thought you should have his name, too."

My own children, neither of whom were in school yet, were chasing or being chased by early arriving Spanish-speaking cousins outside, laughter and squeals the common language they shared. My husband was hoisting rum drinks with anyone and everyone, flogging the five Spanish words he knew to death; his infectious laugh rang through from the patio. *Arroz con pollo*, chicken with rice, simmered on the stove, the warm scent wafting throughout the little home.

"I hope you like your home, your new home," my cousin Ivelisse called out as she passed through the kitchen with a tray of something I couldn't identify on her way out to the patio. "We're so happy to have you with us!"

What a strange twist of fate it had been that I was here.

I was born to parents who weren't married to each other in the early 60s, to a father who was married to someone else and the father of three other children. I only weighed four pounds and change when I was born, despite being full-term, because Nadi had been too afraid to see an obstetrician. My birth grandmother had bundled her into her car in Indiana and forced her to go (in a neighboring town, of course, so her daughter-in-law wouldn't find out).

Over thousands of miles, across decades of time, and against some pretty high odds, I found what adoption search/support groups prefer to call my "first" parents.

Adoptees who have searched will tell you this is a very, very rare occurrence.

Back at the food table, there were lots of things I'd never seen before. As relatives trickled in, many offered small gifts along with acceptance and love in their eyes. They set plates of Puerto Rican staples around the magnificent cake.

Yuca, a potato-like vegetable with a mushier, less dense texture. *Mofongo*, a plantain-based dish traditionally made with the help of a mortar and pestle; this particular version was so heavy on the garlic my eyes watered. *Tostones*, another dish featuring the delectable little banana-like plantain, fried, flattened into discs looking rather like potato pancakes, salted and fried. Rice with a lot of supporting players: *gandules*, or chickpeas, in one pot; pork in another, more chicken in a third. *Alcapurrias*, little fried yuca fritters. Custardy, caramel, melt-in-your-mouth flan, in case the cake wasn't enough dessert.

If food is truly love, my family and I were drowning in love. A different love than the chicken paprikash, goulash, and Hungarian fricassees I was used to, but love nonetheless.

"I heard you were able to meet your father. How did that go?"

The cousin who would become very dear to me, Ivelisse, pulled me to a seat beside her on a couch as the feasting continued. Ivelisse, along with Nadi, was one of our appreciated translators that day. Ivelisse lived in an outer borough of New York City and worked as a nurse; she moved effortlessly between English and Spanish.

"I met him in the airport in Miami," I said, laughing. "It's a long story."

Even today, the story I told to Ivelisse about how Hal tracked down and reached my birthfather a year ago, using just a few scant clues, is another illustration of just how incredibly lucky I have been in my search journey.

I got my birthfather's name, his major in school, and a few other key details about him from Nadi at our first meeting. That's all we had to go on.

Yet another phone call kicked off that aspect of my search, a couple of weeks after I met Nadi. But this time, it was Hal doing the talking, to someone who'd answered the phone at the alumni office of the university where my birthparents first met

"Hey, listen, my siblings and I are throwing a surprise 30th wedding anniversary party for our parents."

Hal found "detective work" fun and interesting. And if anyone could tell a believable yarn on the phone, it was him.

"Everyone in their wedding party went to your school, and we're getting them all to come as an extra surprise for them. We've tracked down all the groomsmen except Lee Satterfield. Do you happen to have any information on where he is now?"

The voice at the other end of the line read off a wealth of information on Lee Satterfield, including his current place of employment.

"They just gave out that information like that? Isn't that illegal or something?" Ivelisse's eyes were saucers.

"This is how things work in the great state of Indiana." I shrugged. "Everything's secret until you catch the right person off guard."

The coincidence Hal discovered next was so improbable that some kind of universal power had to have pulled strings to make things come together.

"Hal's childhood friend was an engineer in the same company as Lee worked in St. Louis," I said to Ivelisse.

Ivelisse laughed.

"God did that for you," she said. "You were meant to find them both, not just your mother."

The rest of the details spilled out.

Hal got Lee's work phone extension number from his boyhood pal. Hal called Lee at work.

"Hi," Hal said, "I know this is going to sound weird, but bear with me for a moment. Did you go to college with a woman named Iluminada Galvez?"

"Yes," Lee replied, very hesitantly.

"My wife is Iluminada's daughter who was given up for adoption. We have reason to believe my wife might be your daughter, too. Could that be the case?"

Hal said he thought the guy hung up. Complete, dead silence.

"Yes, that could definitely be the case," Lee finally answered. "I thought this call would come when she turned twenty-one. I figured when that year came and went, I'd never hear from her."

Ivelisse leaned forward and hugged me.

I told Ivelisse about the first awkward phone call I had with my birthfather later that same day. He wanted to meet me. But he and his wife Carolina—who knew about me, thank goodness—were leaving the country on a trip to visit her relatives. By this time, in the summer of 1992, Hal, the kids and I had already made our move to Florida.

My birthfather asked if we could drive down and meet them at the airport in Miami where they would have a layover before catching their connecting flight abroad.

Hal and I could, and we did.

The reunion was stiff and rather uncomfortable at first, as none of us knew what to say to each other. But that first meeting morphed into a happy family reunion in the summer of 1993, where I met Lee's four other children, and the grandmother who'd taken Nadi under her wing to help make sure I would be born as healthy as possible.

Ivelisse shook her head and smiled after hearing all this. "You never know how things are going to work out," she said.

"Did he really look like Perry Mason?"

Apparently Nadi had mentioned this resemblance to a lot of people once she was courageous enough to share the tale of the daughter who returned from the abyss.

"He's very handsome," I replied, smiling. "And he's very, very smart, like Mami said."

Ivelisse was asking more questions, but I was lost for a moment because I had just called Nadi "Mami" to another person.

My mother Violet had always been "Mama" to me, so referring to Nadi as "Mami" didn't, to me, take anything away from the woman who raised me and loved me.

At that moment, I understood, in my heart I had two mothers.

Ivelisse's sister Adela approached me shortly after the chat with Ivelisse. Adela spoke no English, but her smile was warm and genuine. I understood enough Spanish to know she was welcoming me to the family.

"Köszönöm szépen," I replied without thinking.

I don't know if Adela realized what just happened, since she spoke no English and would have no idea whether what I said was English or something else.

I had responded, automatically, to words in another language in the only other language I knew, Hungarian. I'd said "thank you very much" in what was *my* first language.

I was a farm girl from Indiana, the daughter of a scientist and a school teacher who, by adoption, became the daughter of refugees from World War II, speaking Hungarian to Spanish-speaking relatives on an island two thousand miles away from where I'd grown up.

Talk about a mix of identities.

But, at that moment and from then on, those identities were all mine.

* * *

I came to understand a lot of things a bit more clearly as the years passed and my relationships with the many families whom I called my own would ebb and flow, just as they did with any clan.

Nadi and Raúl moved to the States in the mid 1990's, eventually settling in Jacksonville, Florida. All three of my Puerto Rican brothers and their families ended up there as well. For several years, our families visited each other and spent some holidays together. I received long, warm letters from Nadi during these years—handwritten advice about how to be a good wife, lists of relatives who were coming and going from Puerto Rico, how her other grandchildren were growing and thriving.

She began every letter with "Mi querida Ada," my dear Ada. I never once heard her call me by the name my Hungarian parents had given me.

But life is never static. Change was inevitable.

Hal's and my marriage wouldn't survive forces that pulled it apart ten years after my birth families came into our lives. That is a story for a different time, but I was devastated, cast into an emotional sea that forced me to re-engineer my life and wrestle with some heavy losses.

Raúl passed on in 2002; he had been the glue that helped me bind to Nadi and my brothers. Hal had moved out of our marital home literally two weeks before Raúl's death. I did not cope well.

Traumatized by the divorce, I withdrew further and further into myself. Relationships I should have been nurturing were victims of my pain and hurt, falling sadly by the wayside. Nadi's sons tried to help me. Lee and Carolina were helpful and supportive, but we didn't have the solidity of years together as a family. I loved them all, but I knew some neighbors better than I did these relatives. They didn't know me well, either, and didn't know how to help me.

While I managed to maintain and even strengthen my relationship with Lee, the parent to whom I could ultimately relate the most, my visits and calls to Nadi and that side of the family grew less and less frequent.

Nadi started showing signs of Alzheimer's Disease a few years after Raúl's passing.

During a visit with her in the mid-2000s, we had a conversation that went something like this:

"Mami, I brought you some pictures of your blue-eyed grandchildren."

Nadi had always been tickled by the fact that, among her little tribe of beautiful grandchildren, there were two whose lighter skin and blue eyes made them stand out from the rest. I always referred to my children as the "blue-eyed grandchildren," because normally, that would bring a sly little smile to her face.

This time, it didn't work.

"I have blue-eyed grandchildren? I don't think so. I can't think of any of them who have blue eyes."

"My children do, Mami."

"Your children?"

Heavy, uncomfortable silence.

"I'm your daughter, Mami. I'm Adalee."

Shock, wonder, and tears.

"I gave my daughter away. You're Adalee? How did you come back to me?"

Many more tears and pleas for forgiveness, for the wrong she had done in "giving her baby away to strangers."

Variations of this conversation didn't happen all the time, but they began happening more and more.

I couldn't bear to think that this beautiful soul, my "first" mother, was reliving the pain of relinquishing me for adoption every time she "met" me again. Her recognition of me faded in and out, which was understandable. She hadn't raised me as she had her sons. I was her daughter, yet I was another mother's daughter, too.

I didn't know what to do. I didn't know if I was right in how I was interpreting Nadi's words and actions. The situation was frightening and unnerving to me. All one brother told me was that he thought she might be suffering from depression, though it was acknowledged that she had been prescribed Aricept, a common medication which was often used to stave off the progression of Alzheimer's.

I decided, unilaterally, for better or for worse, that it might be better if I faded back into the abyss from which I had emerged over a decade ago.

And so I did.

* * *

Nadi passed away in 2012. I had not been at her bedside, as her sons had been. They let me know what was happening. But in the end, I couldn't go to her in those last hours. I have no good explanation as to why I couldn't. But it wasn't that I *would not* go. I *could* not.

My now-adult children, and a new partner who entered my life in 2010, accompanied me to the funeral. I was invited, with hugs and warmth, to come to the front of the room where the service was being held, to sit with my brothers. I still knew enough Spanish to know what was being said when my sister-in-law leaned back to explain to some women seated behind us who I was.

"Nadita tuvo una hija?" "Nadi had a daughter?"

Yes, she did.

I am Nadi's daughter.

I am Violet's daughter, too.

EPILOGUE

A family's story never ends, really.

I remain in contact with many of my birth relatives, including my Puerto Rican brothers, their children, and Ivelisse. I see Lee and Carolina, as well as their son and his wife, regularly. Lee and Carolina were at my daughter's wedding and welcomed my daughter's first child, Lee's and Nadi's great-grandchild, in 2018.

I play a lot of roles in my life. I realized, as I've retold this remarkable story, that I've defined myself by those roles for most of my life.

Looking back at these extraordinary chapters, I came to realize I have an identity that goes beyond the roles I play or the families to which I belong or the ethnicities in my heritage.

I wanted to belong to a big family. I ended up belonging to more than one.

I wanted to see and know people who looked like me... people who had some of the same quirks and habits and gestures I did... things I never saw with Shorty and Violet.

I have met, and come to love, a lot of them.

I wanted grandparents, aunts and uncles, and cousins. I have them, and they are mine; I'm not grafted to them by marriage.

I can research on genealogical websites and look at grainy photographs and worn tombstones of people from North Carolina, Kentucky, and Indiana whose blood runs in my veins, too. I can chat in Hungarian on Facebook pages and feel completely at home. I can feel happiness watching the Puerto Rican flag unfurled at a parade and practice my Spanish in the rich Hispanic culture alive in Florida.

I can look at the Stars and Stripes of the United States and be thankful that a lot of people in my past made brave decisions and struck out on daring, frightening adventures so I could be born on American soil.

I can also look back on a childhood and adolescence in which, despite some serious issues, I always knew that I was wanted and loved by the parents who raised me.

But ultimately, I have an identity of my own that is complex, fluid, and unique.

I am me. That's it. Me. I'm a trunk that stands alone, yet surrounded by a forest of beautiful, colorful trees, with different leaves, bark, and branches, but with roots that entwine with mine.

And now, that is what's the most important

ACKNOWLEDGMENTS

Much love and a million thanks to my birth relatives, former in-laws (on paper only, not in my heart), the dear friends who supported me along my search journey, "Hal," the father of my children and the man who was there for me in those years of searching and reunion, and my now grown-up children, whose love and support has been a treasure. I thank the dear colleagues whose stories also appear in this work, for their acceptance and understanding; they are gems buried within my heart. And last but not least, my deepest thanks and forever love to my life partner, beshert (Hebrew for "inevitable, used to describe one's soul mate), beta reader, junk food procurer, and rock when this process of writing and publishing has made me crazy, Keren Vergon. May the joy of all these encounters show me the way to go on.

Figure 3 - Indiana - 1963 - Anna, a little over a year old.

...ndiana - 1967 - About 6 yrs. old, playing dress-up.

Figure 5 – London – June 1985 – Hal proposed to me after my return, and I found out I was adopted the next year, I married him.

RECONCILING

Susana Jiménez-Mueller

PROLOGUE

The countries I lived in and their people left a mark on my persona. I had no control over the political environment in Cuba or how my parents dealt with war and exile. I couldn't change how exile affected a community of refugees, my family, or me.

At home, my sister and I were nurtured and taught by example, the importance of faith, honesty, hard work, education and the strength of a united family.

And then, our world shattered with the death of my father in Union City, New Jersey, eleven months after we arrived in the United States. That was only the beginning of an ever-changing landscape.

COCONUT WATER

1957-1959

Coconut Water
Behind my door, pieces of memories
blend into dreams.
I'm a child, a teen, a woman.
I'm married.

I'm made of the sunshine
that touches the tops of Royal Palms
en mi Patria, and the wind which
pushes on green fronds
and not very sweet coconut water.

I carry the fragrance of Cuban coffee
and hot buttered bread on my skin.
    Susana Jiménez-Mueller

Photographs bring me snippets of *mi Cuba*, my Cuba. Birthday parties with cake, *bocaditos*, tea sandwiches, and soda. The coolness of the tiled house in December, a romantic print on the wall, a single bulb hanging from the ceiling without a shade over the kitchen table, an open window or door.

The first four years of my life were like a slow-moving river before it picked up speed, ready to plunge as a waterfall. During this time, our family went about daily living with hope in the economic and political future of Cuba.

My sister Gloria 'Glori,' twelve years my senior and the beneficiary of my adoration, attended *la secundaria,* junior high school. She came and went, smartly dressed in her uniform, carrying a pile of books. She lit up the room with her bright smile, and her hips swayed like a soft rolling wave as she walked. I wanted to be like her and wear the yellow uniform scarf which denoted her current schoolyear.

By age three, I pestered my mother, Martina, to take me to school. She pleaded my case to the headmistress at a nearby kindergarten who allowed me to attend half days a few days a week. I couldn't believe I was in school and I got to wear Glori's yellow scarf from the previous year!

Everyone in the kindergarten was much older than me, and I became their toy doll. An exemplary, well-behaved student, I proudly wore my good conduct medal on Fridays. Sometimes, right before lunch, Dad would pick me up on his bicycle, his white short sleeve shirt reflecting the sunlight. I sat in the front metal basket like a queen hugging my knees to my chest. The narrow streets and sidewalks blurred as we rode by, then finally came into focus when we arrived home.

Other days were filled with grocery shopping at the corner *bodega,* grocery store, with my mother, playing alone, or with my neighbor Maritza. Once, Maritza and I dressed up as cabaret dancers with tricolor crinoline petticoats stuffed in the front of our panties and the rest of the slip netting puffed over our derrieres. Topless, we danced an imagined *comparsa,* a dance with musicians during carnival, along the sidewalk, all the way to the end of the block. Our escapade ended when we were caught by my mother, and then my bottom wore the redness of a spanking.

On weekdays, Mom managed the household rhythm. Family tradition dictated that by four o'clock kids were bathed and ready for a snack, before dads came home. Such was the case in our home and by five, I watched cartoons, sitting in my big-girl oak rocking chair, a miniature replica of the one in our living room. My father, Orlando, would arrive from work, ready for family time later in the afternoon.

Dad, an entrepreneur, sold small home appliances and goods. His inventory and his bicycle, "the delivery truck," occupied part of our living room.

Although Santa Clara was not a small town, our extended family lived only blocks away from each other. Uncles, aunts, and cousins visited regularly, dropping in for una *tacita de café,* a small cup of coffee, and a chat. On Sundays, we attended church, then family and friends strolled around the Leóncio Vidal Park, at the center of town.

In December of 1958, the tempo of life changed in expectation of revolutionary forces entering the city. My parents told me there would be no Christmas that year and Santa Claus didn't exist. I wasn't upset by this bit of information.

Santa Clara turned lifeless that Christmas as people kept to themselves. We locked our home and moved to a small apartment in a *pasaje*, breezeway, on Colón Street close to Aunt Maria, waiting for the rumored attack by Fidel Castro's revolutionary forces. Fidel sent Ché Guevara, an Argentine Marxist revolutionary, and his right-hand man, to capture the city and divide the island in half to improve his chance of winning the revolution. Conflicting information about the progress of the rebel forces confused the general public. Nevertheless, our extended family prepared for the imminent attack by storing food and moving to more secure homes or away to the countryside with relatives.

Early on the morning of the 29th of December, Ché Guevara delivered his assault on the city. Amidst skirmishes around town, the second rebel column, led by Rolando Cubela, commanded the frontal attack to the police station located across from the old *Parque del Carmen*, Del Carmen Park, where the city was founded hundreds of years before. For three days the town remained in darkness, terrorized by the sound of gunshots and Molotov cocktails exploding. Santa Clara surrendered on December 31st. Cuba was entering a time of change, and so was I.

Cautiously we returned home to the ebb and flow of daily life. I was back in kindergarten, and that February I participated in the school's carnival celebration with mums in my hair and dressed in yellow and black—like a Chinese girl. Mom made the costume, and Glori took care of my makeup and hair. She and I were becoming inseparable.

Our parents continued to be alert to the changes in the country and recognized the intangible signs of communism. Their deliberation, not openly discussed with anyone outside our home, resulted in a plan to use South America as a stepping stone to exile in the United States.

A year after the revolution, we embarked on our journey to Venezuela where Uncles Máximo and Fermín and their families were established since the early 1950s. My world faded as I watched neighbors stripping our home. Everything was sold except my rocking chair.

We left Cuba that same week, December 17, 1959, on the *Virginia Churruca*, a Spanish passenger ship, and arrived Christmas week. Getting all the packages in Uncle Máximo's white Ford proved impossible, and he wanted to throw away my rocking chair, the only thing I had left from home.

No!

Dad, knowing my attachment, figured out the way to save the chair was to remove the rockers. The trunk, bulged with boxes, suitcases, and my maimed chair, was secured with a rope in a series of loops around the rear bumper.

As night fell, we headed inland to San Felipe on the two-way narrow winding mountain road, a four-hour trip in those days. Mom held me tight every time a large bus or truck passed us exclaiming under her breath, "*¡Ay Dios mío!* Oh my God!"

We drove south, hugging the face of the mountain, and arrived in San Felipe sometime after midnight. A doll as tall as me—a gift from my aunt and uncle—waited on the kitchen table. Sadness flooded my heart. They didn't love me enough to buy a doll that looked like me!

San Felipe was a melting pot with residents from Europe, the Middle East, Asia, and Cuba. I drifted in and out of melancholy for a while as I adapted to my new surroundings—a new house, looming mountains, cold mornings, and hot afternoons. I grew to love my doll and became accustomed to diversity.

My parents rented a colonial house and the living room became a bodega. Just like in Cuba, our home doubled as a warehouse. This time, the inventory was sugar in twenty-five-pound bags piled five feet high, my sugar mountain. I climbed the sugar mountain when I wanted alone time, to read or sing.

The traditions brought from the old country clashed with the customs in Venezuela. Specifically, the local population of San Felipe viewed industrious Cubans as job snatchers. It was a time of uncertainty for the adults where graffiti was a daily reminder of local distrust. For me, it was a time of awe. On Sunday mornings I ate French bread with *Brün,* Danish canned butter, went to the movies to watch the latest *Lone Ranger* and *El Zorro* episodes with Dad, and had a gelato after the morning matinee. Later, in the coolness of the evening mountain air, our small family strolled in the main plaza during *la retreta,* the open-air band concert where immigrants became a community, playing instruments from their homeland.

President Kennedy was shot in November of 1963, and Dad commented that perhaps it wasn't such a good idea to move to America after all.

I heard Mom say, "It´s the best move we have. You've said in the past, and I agreed that sooner or later, the United States will be the only free country in the Western Hemisphere. We must stay on course."

In 1963, Dad sold the grocery store, and we went to the capital to wait for the U.S. Embassy appointment and our visas. In Caracas, we lived in *El Hotel Comercio* for an entire month where I was treated like a V.I.P. Every morning the kitchen staff prepared buttered toast cut in three long crunchy pieces, and I ate my breakfast at the dining room bar.

The visas weren't granted because the adults didn't have jobs waiting in the United States. In great disappointment, we returned to San Felipe where Dad opened a smaller grocery store. This time we didn´t share our home with the new bodega, and I was told we needed to curb spending.

That year, the family focus was to replenish savings in preparation for the trip and secure work letters, the last requirement to gain entry visas to the United States. Cousin Pedro who lived in Union City, New Jersey, offered to secure work letters for my parents and sister, and by the end of 1963, the embassy granted visas. The bags were packed and we were ready for our trip to America

CAN I LEARN TO WALK WITHOUT YOU?

1964-1967

Can I Learn to Walk Without You?
Being nine—it was yesterday.
My hand in yours ...
In winter, early spring, and summer we walked
but not as much that autumn.

Turning leaves, crisp air, Halloween.
New experiences without you.
Where are you? I wondered.

If only I had known you would be gone
with the first snow.
November 25, 1964.
*   Susana Jiménez-Mueller*

The plans to move to America culminated when we disembarked in Ft. Lauderdale in January of 1964. Cousin Manolito waited for us at the port and drove us to a downtown Miami hotel. The hotel room, with the scent of many travelers, included a coin-operated radio on an old night table.

A couple days later, equipped with heavy winter clothes purchased at a Salvation Army store, we left Miami on a two-tiered Greyhound bus. Somewhere at a North Carolina truck stop, later that day, Glori and I sat with our parents drinking hot chocolate and eating our first apple pie. The thick, cakey crust covered gooey chunks of cooked apples - I can still remember the smell and taste.

The rest of the trip took us through isolated farmland with houses dressed in Christmas lights. Hugging herself, Mom commented, looking out into the silver night, "See those houses with their little lights? They seem sad. I never liked the loneliness of *el campo*, the countryside."

We arrived in New York City in the evening after twenty-four hours on the road. The snow inside the bus terminal looked like my sugar mountain. I walked into a refrigerated wonderland and could see my breath! Unfortunately, the large green army coat didn't keep me warm.

Cousin Pedro waited at the terminal and after high-spirited greetings, our bags were collected, and we were off to Cousin Cheo's apartment in Union City. We took the Lincoln Tunnel to New Jersey. The clumps of dirty snow along the tunnel walls reflected the lights from passing cars and filtered through the curling smoke coming from Dad and Cousin Pedro's cigarettes.

We walked into the building, past the host of bare trees with twisted branches hanging low from the weight of frozen water, and up the stairs into the apartment single file. After more greetings, hugs, and kisses, we shed our winter wear. The heat—dry and suffocating—assaulted my lungs. I sat on the sofa by a frosted window, struggling to identify the outline of a swing set blanketed with snow. The swing set struck a comparison to the hammock hung in Uncle Máximo's backyard in San Felipe.

The next morning, Dad rented an apartment on Bergenline Avenue and enrolled me in fourth grade at Roosevelt Elementary School. He taught me how to get to school, located just a few blocks away, and on my first day, gave me a kiss and turned me over to the vice principal who escorted me to class.

The teacher met us at the door and made a gesture I understood to mean shed my coat. I entered the long dimly lit cloak room, and the smell of muddy boots overpowered my senses. I hung my coat and shoved the gloves into one of the pockets then followed her to the front of class. She introduced me, butchering my surname; Jiménez turned into Gemini. I wished Dad, who was bilingual, could have stayed with me.

Twenty plus pairs of eyes stared at me as I stood in front of the teacher's desk. Her hand fell lightly on my shoulder and she pointed to a seat by the heat register, under the wide window. I took my seat, glancing at the row of two-story houses across the street.

Fresh snow fell mid-morning, and when the alarm bell rang dismissing class for lunch, we ran out of school eager to get home. Walking on fresh snow, I became disoriented and backtracked, relieved to spot a familiar landmark, the corner bar on Bergenline Avenue.

At school, I couldn't understand the posted signs or how to say I needed to go to the bathroom. I learned by imitating others: take out a paper, fold it in half, number one through ten every other line and eleven through twenty on the opposite side, write your name and date on the upper right-hand corner, and take the spelling test—except I didn't know the words. There were rules, so many rules at school. While in class, the teacher didn't allow Cousin Tony, who spoke fluent English, to translate for me, which increased my sense of isolation.

I liked it when we went to the school library. I felt safe sitting at the dark wooden table by the arched window, surrounded by books. I didn't need to talk to anyone.

On Valentine's Day, kids exchanged little cards folded in half, stuffed in tiny envelopes. I received many but didn't reciprocate because I didn't know I should bring cards for everyone. Who makes all these rules? A wave of heat traveled from my throat, engulfing my cheeks. I sank low in my desk among curious glances and imagined them laughing at me. I wanted the earth to open up and swallow me.

Later that month, crying inconsolably, I refused to go to school. The frustration broke an emotional floodgate. *I'm not going back to school!*

My parents tried to figure out how to manage the situation, and in the interim, Tuesday came and also Wednesday. On Friday, a hard knock at the door made my heart jump. Mom didn´t open it because she couldn't understand the truant officer.

The officer returned with Cousin Margie, Cheo's daughter, who attended the same school but in a higher grade. Mom opened the door to a man dressed in blue, personifying authority. I couldn't escape or hide.

The interrogation began while Margie interpreted, "Why aren't you in school?"

And then to my mother, "Do you understand it's against the law to keep a child at home?"

Mom stood taller than her five-foot-one stature, legs apart in a protective stance, and said, "She can't communicate and feels isolated and sad. The teacher won't allow Tony to help her. She refuses to go back to school."

Margie translated her response.

"Who is Tony?" the officer asked Margie.

After much discussion, the officer said he would talk to the principal to see what could be done. Nevertheless, I needed to be in school the following Monday.

Margie interceded for me as well as my parents and other cousins. The teacher agreed Tony could help me navigate the rules and translate for me. Seated beside him, words slowly grew familiar, and I taught others how to do long division – Math was my language.

On Sundays, our extended family often came together for a meal at one of our relative's homes. Dad's cousin, Guillermo, an architect who lived in Manhattan, would visit. Cousin Manuel, from Venezuela and in the States attending college in a nearby town, also joined us. Mostly, the New Jersey cousins gathered to discuss the situation in Cuba, politics and in general catch up on the week's activities. The men always dressed in smart suits with ties and the women in dresses. Mom wore her pearl necklace, and my parents tended to each other, with a smile or brief touch of a hand.

St. Patrick's Day came, and everyone in school dressed in green. I had an army green coat and gloves, so I didn't feel left out. Later that day, I walked down the block to the bakery with my sister to buy cupcakes decorated with little men called leprechauns. Eating green cupcakes took me straight to heaven. I must admit, everything tasted better in forty-degree temperature.

A new baby blue polyester coat arrived with spring. No more army coat! On my way to school, I strolled by tulips and other flowers which had sprung from the chilly ground in front of homes, and my spirits lifted.

At the end of the school year, I still couldn't speak the language and didn't move up to fifth grade, but counted to one hundred for my father as we strolled along Bergenline Avenue with its brightly lit store windows.

I made friends with Susy, the building superintendent's daughter, and we played in her tiny backyard behind the apartment building. One hot summer day in June, the sky suddenly turned dark in what looked like a solar eclipse, and we ran inside scared, looking for our parents thinking the world was ending.

The summer of 1964 brought other challenges in the form of chickenpox, a fire in our apartment building, and Dad's hospitalization and cancer diagnosis.

I turned ten in September and welcomed fall and a new school year. In the evenings, my sister and I helped Mom cut embroidered roses from yards of cloth. The first time she handed me the scissors, she said, "Be careful. We have to pay ten cents for each one we ruin." The heavy scissors and her admonition weighed in my hand as I struggled to cut away each pink rose from its netting foundation. On Halloween, we didn't cut material. Instead, I dressed as a clown and trick-or-treated for the first time while Glori documented the experience.

The streets came alive in colors of crimson and gold with leaves tumbling in the wind. Dad spent most of his days in bed, and I only ventured in once in a while to see him, his frame thinning, cancer eating away his life and ours. One evening, I watched television on the pull-out sofa, and Mom asked me to turn off the set. I didn't comply. Dad gathered enough strength and left the bedroom to confront me.

"Turn off the T.V. You pay attention to your mother. Listen to me. I'm not dead yet!"

Those words stayed with me throughout my life, keeping me on the straight and narrow.

Mom nursed him, and on November 25th, she asked me to come in and say goodbye to him. He had lost his eyesight and his frail body looked like that of an Auschwitz victim. He raised his hand slightly to hand me a small piece of thin onion velum paper. The note said for me to go to Cousin Berta's, be a good girl, and that he would see me soon. My parents must have planned the farewell weeks earlier when he could see to write the note.

I lay on the mattress in Berta's living room watching the red sky, knowing it would snow, and I felt him leave us. He died that evening.

Mom landed in the hospital days after the funeral with a jaundice attack, and Glori moved us closer to the hospital. That meant a different school district and learning my way around a new school. I joined the class just in time for a Christmas gift exchange, and I brought crayons and a coloring book as a gift. In dismay and embarrassment, I saw the girl's look of disdain as she opened my present. I wanted the earth to swallow me – again.

Mom came home right before Christmas, and we tended to her. Another move in January and back at Bergenline Avenue and the familiarity of the last neighborhood and school. The first-floor studio apartment had a heat register that couldn't keep up with the frigid nights. The three of us slept in the same bed with every coat we owned piled on top to ward off the cold nights.

Uncle Pedro, Mom's brother, arrived from Venezuela and came to see her every day for lunch. Despite his visits being a great solace, she decided to move us to Miami, where we could survive without speaking the language. That winter, we escaped the cold and dark dreary days but didn't give up on the dream of a future in America.

We lived in southwest Miami, where Cubans coped with changes and exile. They called it "La Sawesera." Mom worked in a factory sewing zippers, I attended Riverside Elementary School, and Glori's fight with Lupus re-emerged as a result of stress after our father's death. For my sister, hospital stays became frequent as she managed physical pain.

I became an avid reader and retreated to make-believe worlds, often reading in bed by the light of a full moon, dreaming of a better life for us.

Although my aunts and uncles in Venezuela helped us emotionally and economically, we struggled to make ends meet, treading water during our first three years in our second exile.

During the summer of 1967, I spent a week at Cousin Manolito and his wife Edith's home in Hialeah. I rode on a wooden roller coaster at a fair, had ice cream and hamburgers, and slept in bunk beds with their kids. Unbeknownst to me, the monetary situation at home reached a climax. There was no money to purchase groceries. Glori, who was feeling better after receiving multiple cortisone treatments, concocted a plan and partnered with a neighbor to host an apartment building party. Each family contributed a dollar, and everyone could have plenty of leftover food. The idea was ingenious. Glori was great that way.

I returned home the following weekend to a building buzzing with music and laughter. Mom had made *arroz con pollo,* chicken and yellow rice, sweet plantains, salad, and there were plenty of refreshments. Before we went to bed, Glori told me how the party came to be and that I had been "sent away" because there was no food in the house.

Enraged, I said to my mother and sister, "Never again. You don't send me away. Never!"

In December 1967, as the war in Vietnam raged and constant news of a chaotic world flooded the media and entered our home through the television and radio, we returned to Venezuela seeking the security of our extended family.

Slowly, I was learning to walk without my father.

GUAVA ICE CREAM

1968-1969

Being Thirteen
I hold the frosty blue aluminum tumbler
slowly savoring each bite.
And ponder my entire life in that moment,
wondering what is right.
    Susana Jiménez-Mueller

Half a year passed since we moved back to the protection of our extended family in Venezuela to care for my sister's health and survive as a nuclear family. The plan didn't work. We couldn't find a doctor there to keep Glori's lupus at bay. Therefore, my sister, now twenty-five, returned to the U.S. seeking treatment for her latest bout of illness. Mom and I stayed behind for me to finish the school year.

I was thirteen when she and I moved to the rental house in San Felipe. She chose the neighborhood for its proximity to my high school, *El Liceo Aristides Rojas*. The streets were clean and the architecture reminiscent of a colonial era and our Santa Clara. The houses shared a wall, painted in different unmuted colors. Slanted, they leaned against each other, rooted in the mountain slope beneath them. Our humble rental had two bedrooms, a living room, an open-air dining room with an adjacent kitchen, and a small backyard with a big tree. My bedroom window faced 14th street.

Since Dad's death, Mom had been consumed with fighting Glori's illness, and now for the first time I had her all to myself. It felt odd to have personal attention in a world reduced to school and sometimes visiting family and friends. For the most part, aside from Uncle Máximo's daily visits and Glori's letters, there weren't any distractions. We had a radio, but no television or phone.

It was 1969 and we had put a man on the moon, yet in this house it might have well been the early 1900s, with depressing lighting not meant for reading. I missed reading mysteries and going to the school library. I missed the U.S.

In this human condition, homemade guava ice cream waited for me in a blue aluminum tumbler every day after school. Mom never missed a day of making ice cream, and I always anticipated getting home for the treat. Years later, she told me she was making up for lost time with me. Looking back, being alone with my mother was an opportunity to observe how she handled a potentially dangerous situation, and a second sticky one.

The first lesson began late one night.

Crash!

I bolted upright in bed with enough time to see the rock's trajectory ending on the floor a couple feet from me. The street light invading my window turned the jagged edges of the broken window into a prism.

Mom ran in whispering, "Are you all right? Come quickly. Move away from the window."

She then called out her brother's name loudly, "*¡Máximo levantate, ven pronto!* Máximo get up, come quickly!"

Mom was using my uncle's name as a security deterrent and wanted the attackers to think there was a man in the house. Instantly, my dog barked, waking up the rest of the neighborhood. Without turning on the lights, we went down the hallway to her bedroom and sat on the bed.

She leaned close to me, "It's time we make friends."

Make friends with whom?

I already knew some of the kids who lived down the street from us because every day we rode to school on a *por puesto*, a taxi with a fare charged per seat. In the *claroscuro*, between shadow and light, of the room, my puzzled look reached her.

She continued, "We are strangers in this land, a widow and a young teenager. We're the perfect target for ignorant people. People who hate us for being Cuban and know we've lived in the U.S." Taking a breath, she said, "Your uncles are men of great economic importance in this community. They're not liked because there's a perception Cubans have taken jobs away from Venezuelans. Your dad and I owned the grocery store on 3rd Avenue in 1962, and graffiti on the walls read 'Cubans go home!'"

"I'm scared of going to school tomorrow. I don't know who hates me," I said.

She responded, "You'll stay home. Come, let's make some *atol*." Atol was our ancestral pre-Colombian drink made with milk, cornstarch, and sugar. We drank the hot, thick, sweet beverage and slept together. The following day we moved my bed into her room.

Right after lunch, she washed her face and ran a comb through her wavy, thinning, salt and pepper hair, then set four demitasses on the peltre tray and filled them with espresso.

"Mom, what are you doing?"

"I'm going to pay a visit to the COPEI men and introduce ourselves. Come open the door for me."

When she alluded to "making friends," she meant befriending the men at the COPEI headquarters—only two houses north of ours. COPEI, *El Comité de Organización Política Electoral Independiente* or The Independent Political Electoral Organization Committee. They expounded a Christian democratic political ideology which advocated for a commitment to social market principles and qualified interventionism, code words for socialism.

I watched my mother step out into the hot afternoon, cross the street, and approach the men sitting on the front doorsteps of the green house. My throat tightened as she offered them the drink. The two men invited her inside. I heard them say, "*Entre doña.* Come in, ma'am."

It felt like an eternity until I saw her figure slowly descending the steps to the narrow sidewalk. Back home, she told me she introduced herself as a Christian and *la viuda* de Orlando Jimenez, Orlando Jimenez's widow. She explained we were living alone, and our house was stoned the previous night, adding I could've been hurt. She had noticed her words were not a surprise to them. She won them over with rhetoric and asked for their protection. My mother walked into the wolf's den and survived!

Later on, I became the courier of bananas and other fruits from Uncle Máximo's farm which Mom always set aside for our "guardians."

Instead of more rocks through my window, I was serenaded one night by a young man who worked for another uncle. We never figured out how he knew where we lived, except that as a family, we were being surveilled.

The second lesson began on a Wednesday in July.

Uncle Máximo arrived in his farm garb, all the way down to his muddy black boots, happy. He brought a live chicken and a hunger for stew. Framing the door with his short figure, his belly cinched in a black buckled belt, he offered the flapping feathered gift with extended arms and said, "Here you go Marta. Make me a fricassee for tomorrow's lunch."

Horrified, Mom said, "*¿Estas loco?* Are you crazy? I haven't killed a chicken in years!"

Taken aback by her response, he said, "It's like riding a horse. You just don't forget."

Uncle Máximo tied the splendid white specimen to the water faucet in the courtyard a few feet from the dog, a bad idea. Terri had never seen a chicken before and growled, *Intruder, intruder, alert, alert.* Tied to the oak tree, he fought the restraining leash and howled, *Let me loose! I'll catch it for you.*

Lacking any preparation, Mom and I stepped up to the courtyard. Pointing to the chicken she said, "Sue, bring me the chicken. I'm ready."

I approached the fowl slowly. I figured I would launch myself on the creature and grab it around the chest, far away from its pointy beak.

The chicken, sensing its future, squawked and pulled at the thin string holding her to the faucet, trying to take flight with one scaly yellow foot in the air, the other well-grounded. The agitated Terri pulled at his leash so hard he stood on his hind legs, howling, *I mean it.*

I want it!

In one mighty leap the bird took flight, breaking her bondage. I chased it, zig-zagging through the small backyard, trying to catch her every time she leaped in the air. Low clouds of dust rose behind us.

Mom yelled instructions, "Hurry, grab it. To your left. Run, run."

I chased the chicken and, dizzy in her escape, she flew right into Terri. He broke his leash and grabbed her by the neck, then shook it back and forth. I reached Terri and slapped him on the butt, surprising him, and for a brief moment, he dropped the chicken. I grabbed it. The barking dog, Mom yelling, round and round we went. The bird's heart pounded through her feathers, right on my hand.

I delivered the chicken to its awful fate and held on to Terri.

Hesitating, Mom took the chicken by the neck and spun it in the air screaming with each swing, "I can't do it. I can't do it. I can't do it."

By the third time, she let go of the bird in mid-air.

The chicken landed sideways and stood up staggering. Terri escaped my grasp and went after it, but Mom stood between the dog and the bird, like a football player ready to intercept. I grabbed Terri and tied him back to the tree.

On Thursday, Uncle Máximo arrived salivating, when to his dismay there was no chicken fricassee. That day he ate a lunch of fried eggs, white rice, and sweet plantains.

His last words as he left the house were, "Tomorrow fricassee, right? I know you can do this."

In the afternoon, after more dog barking and chicken chasing, Mom killed the chicken, and the smell of blood drove the dog into wolf-like spasms.

The next steps were to boil the water, dip the chicken in the hot pot, and pluck the feathers. How can this bird have so many feathers? I counted ten, twenty, thirty feathers as a white carpet spread around our feet.

Then wash the chicken, dress the chicken, sauté the onions and pepper; add the cumin, garlic, salt, and a can of tomato sauce; add the potatoes; make the rice; and fry the plantains.

The table was set for one. Uncle Máximo arrived and entered the kitchen taking in the savory smells. "Aren't you joining me for lunch?"

Mom responded, "Oh, we ate already. Sorry. We were so hungry."

He sat down to his lunch, and we kept him company. After the first bite, the grin on his face gave tribute to the chicken that gave her life for his stew. Lunch ended.

After he left, Mom and I looked at each other, and without saying a word, she went to the kitchen, took the black pot by both handles, and served the dog the chicken fricassee.

Mom and I lived together for six months before she traveled to the United States at the end of that year to help Glori. My sister, ill and alone in Miami, dealing with hospitals, doctors, and treatments needed our mother more than me.

I remained under my godparent's care, Uncle Máximo and his wife Luisa, to finish the school year. I cried myself to sleep every night, processing the loneliness of my predicament. During the day, though, anchored in the memories created during the previous months with my mother, I harnessed her strength, shaping the woman I would become.

NO ORANGES FOR YOU

1974-1975

Oranges
In the warmth of eternal summer
the taste of orange juice
is no more.
  Susana Jiménez-Mueller

In the early seventies, at the edge of an idyllic American television-like life was our Cuban immigrant community, which served *café con leche*, coffee and milk, hot buttered bread for breakfast and savory lunches with an abundance of beans, rice, and plantains. In the afternoons, when not at college, I sipped sweet espresso and enjoyed listening to recordings of *Pototo y Filomeno*, an old Cuban comedy duo on the local Cuban radio station. On most days, you heard the comedians' voices overlaid with laughter coming from other studio apartments.

In January of 1974, we lived on Flagler Street across from my Alma Mater, Miami Senior High School, surrounded by my native language.

We bought groceries on credit, including meat from the nearby Cuban bodega which always had fresh gladiolas for sale in a bucket of water placed near the front door. The Navarro drugstore on 16th Avenue sold familiar remedies like cod liver oil, *Numoticine*, Coty facial powder, and Agustin Reyes Royal Violets cologne. The gasoline station on 27th Avenue was Cuban owned, and they treated me like family. Even the laundromat next door to the gas station had signs in Spanish and smelled of fresh fruit.

On Saturdays, my American ritual included waking up late, buying orange juice and a dozen Krispy Kreme doughnuts at Zagamys, a Jewish grocery store down the road on 23rd Avenue. No Spanish signs there.

One day, I arrived from Zagamys with my treasure and sat with my sister at the green speckled Formica table in our tiny kitchen. It was mid-morning, and Mom had her back to us, her apron snug around her form-fitting dress. She always dressed in a skirt or dress and her feet in sling back wedge shoes, white in the summertime and black in winter. She was *montando los frijoles para el almuerzo,* starting the bean soup for lunch, and didn't pay attention to our conversation.

The acrid smell of black beans filled the air as they started to boil with their spices—*ajo, cebolla, comino y ají.* Ah, yes…garlic, onion, cumin, and green pepper. The different smells fought each other for air space and mixed with the mildly humid breeze entering through the back door. It was difficult to breathe the thick aromatic air, but I continued drinking my juice and taking huge bites from the doughnut, mindfully catching the cloudy crystallized sugar flakes in mid-air.

I ate, half-listening to Glori tell us about school buses full of Cubans who went to the packing houses in Homestead on Saturdays to wash and grade oranges.

"Easy work," she said. "Definitely easier than washing dishes or cleaning houses." Glori was alluding to the many Cuban professionals still jump-starting their lives.

As she spoke, I pictured doctors in their white coats washing dishes, busing tables, and cleaning houses instead of attending the sick. I recalled this information was part and parcel of everyday life. One could often catch someone exclaiming on a bus, "Did you hear doctor so and so, the best in Santa Clara has opened a practice on Flagler Street? He doesn't have to wash dishes at the Fountain Blue Hotel anymore!" These conversations always ended in, "If they can do it, so can we. We can all succeed in this country."

Pulling me back to reality, Glori said, "Come on, let's all go. It'll be fun, and we'll get paid a few dollars and bring home some oranges. My friend Lucia told me she goes all the time, and it's a blast."

"Okay, I will go."

Why did I just agree? Am I on a sugar high?

142

Excited at the prospect of an adventure, Glori continued to explain how we would travel to the packing house. I half-heard something about an old school bus picking us up near Miami High. I had no idea what I was getting into.

I said, "Well, you figure out the details. Let me do the laundry before lunchtime." I kissed Mom and took off with her grocery store cart, heavy with clothes separated in pillowcases; quarters and dimes jingling in my shorts pocket. I couldn't wait to own a washing machine and be rid of the cart.

I couldn't wait to live like an American.

The following Saturday arrived soon enough, and in the fog of sleep, I turned and reached for the thin sheet to cover my face, trying to hide from the kitchen light flooding the apartment. It was still dark outside, and a rooster crowed near the front door as the smell of freshly brewed coffee invaded my dream. I wondered how the chicken had gotten away from the *santero*, a priest of the Cuban Santería religion, and the owner of the motel-converted-to-studio apartments where we lived.

Eyes still shut, I inched to the edge feeling for the sneakers under the bed. I found them, rolled out of bed, and shuffled to the bathroom to get ready. Mom was busy in the kitchen preparing lunches. There would be no visit to Zagamys today.

The three of us crossed Flagler Street in the soft morning light and joined other women heading for the bus. Many of them wore big rollers under head kerchiefs, and the fragrance of Dippity Do hair gel emanated from their wet hair. They were colorful, walking in pairs, chatting, purses hanging from the crook of their arms, and lunch cantinas swinging in their hands. Some wore dresses, but most wore pants.

We reached the run-down yellow school bus, and I sat toward the middle at a window. Mom sat beside me and Glori to her right. I was there in body but not spirit. I felt a stranger amongst these people, and yet I'm sure others driving alongside our bus that day saw a girl with olive skin, hair pulled back under a kerchief, and a portion of a sleeveless blouse—just another Cuban.

We rambled south on dusty US 1 as the women sang songs and men told stories from *La Patria*, the homeland, and the hated Fidel Castro, Cuba's tyrant. Glori's voice rose and blended with others in the sweetness of the moment. Mom quietly looked out the window, and I sat there watching them, forever stuck between two cultures.

We arrived at the packing house and made our way through tall itchy grass. The scent of citrus invaded every pore as we walked into the damp building with its large open windows which didn't provide ventilation.

The foreman, a tall red-faced man dressed in jeans, wearing a large hat, came barking orders. The bus leader translated the barks, "Go to the bathroom if you need to. Hurry up and find your places. No open purses under the conveyor belt."

Lucia leaned over to Glori and whispered, "The rejected oranges will go in the empty box under the belt." Glori's half-hearted smile indicated she now understood the ramifications of this adventure, and the fun she had promised me would not crystallize.

I felt humiliated, but more so, incensed.

Mom looked calm. This wasn't the first time she had been hollered at, looked at sideways, or even spat upon. She became numb to atmospheres similar to the hot sweatshop where she sewed hundreds of zippers a day, working by the clock, under the eye of a floor supervisor.

We took our places, and oranges started tumbling down the conveyors, soaked in chlorine water. Some hands in yellow gloves and others naked moved in compass to the rumbling of the machinery, a count of four by four. Like window wipers, hands lightly brushed the tops of the fruit, sometimes swiftly stopping to pluck one and throw it in the box under the belt. We didn't bring gloves.

The job was to choose United States Department of Agriculture quality fruit by feel and sight. What did I know about choosing quality fruit? The closest I had ever been to this much fruit was at my Aunt Celia's house in Venezuela when she prepped guavas to make *casquitos de guayaba*, guava shells in syrup. If I were visiting, I would be drafted to peel the tiny fruits.

After a few minutes of pushing the oranges around, the stench of chlorine filled my nostrils and burned my eyes. I began to sneeze. Leaning over, I told Mom we needed to stop. The foreman towered over me and said to shut up and work. To which I replied, "No. This water has too much chlorine, it's not safe."

Turning to my family, I spoke in Spanish, pleading for them to step away from the line, but they continued working. His flushed face, inches from mine, stared at me in disbelief. I continued to explain that as a chemistry major in college, I recognized the unsafe process.

He said, "You are not getting paid, and the bus is not going to take you back now. No oranges for you!"

I responded, "That's fine. I will sit on the steps." Turning around, I said to my mother, "*Madre, no te preocupes, yo me siento en los escalones y espero.* Don't worry Mom, I will sit on the steps and wait."

The wooden floor planks echoed as I made way to the front steps. Reaching the handrail, I turned and watched the lovely women and men, their hands moving in rhythm. Oranges tumbled under their hands, jumped, and landed, by the impetus of the fruits behind them. A wave of orange. I would never look at produce the same way, and orange juice would never taste the same.

Slowly the heat of the morning escalated, vaporizing the dew left on the wild grass. I became engulfed in my own thoughts of future success. I had all day. I took out the small spiral pocket notepad from my purse and worked on my five-year plan. The plan to break from the mold I had been poured into by the American eye because I looked and sounded different. A woman who they assumed would get married, have a ton of children, and become a burden to society. I refused to be cast in this role.

I skimmed the notepad page as I reviewed the bulleted list, my plan of emancipation. The list included becoming an American citizen by the end of the year, working in the college chemistry lab until I graduated the following year with an AA in Chemistry, and then

145

earning a Bachelor's of Science in Chemistry by 1977. The road to emancipate my family and me was firmly written and forecasted.

I leaned back on the steps, stretched, and contemplated the rural setting when I heard the rising crescendo of my compatriots as the conveyor belts halted.

Mom, Glori, and bus cohorts visited me during the morning, lunch, and afternoon breaks. At lunch, Mom's ham and cheese sandwiches on Wonder Bread chased by a bit of coffee still hot from the thermos never tasted better.

The bus returned late in the afternoon, and everyone piled back on, each carrying a bag of disqualified oranges. The sweaty bodies slouched in their seats on the long bumpy ride home, drained by the heat and without voices left to sing.

I imagined freedom from stereotypes and couldn't wait to reach home, my safe place.

LOVE AND THE BEADED COIN PURSE

1975-1985

Never Fear
Of two souls, the light does burn.
Over paths, I remember now,
I crisscross every turn.
Recalling tender summer nights,
above congested street lights
on our throne of dreams and future sights.
Just being happy.
I am not sad
for the time we aren't near.
We will meet the test and grow stronger.
Never fear my dear.
    Jon Mueller

Mom's small, sparsely beaded coin purse defied the laws of physics. If the week was prosperous, it felt light on Fridays, entrusted with a wad of bills—the culmination of her pay at the sweatshop near the Miami Airport. Soon, the coin purse bulged with change, and we were back to buying food on credit from the bodega and counting coins to make sure I had enough money to buy gas to get to school.

In 1975 I still lived at home. Not because I didn't have a desire to strike out on my own, but from a sense of responsibility to the family and to improve our standard of living. By now, Glori's lupus had complicated her health, and she was on dialysis.

I was twenty-one, enrolled in college, worked in the chemistry lab, and on my way to reaching my dreams. My earnings were added to Mom's coin purse every week. She held the purse strings, and that was okay. One for all and all for one. Our extended family called us the three musketeers.

The first two years of college went by swiftly amid studying groups, tests, and work. By the end of 1975, I finished my associate's degree, and the beaded coin purse could always be found, among pencils in the beige kitchen drawer.

With school out for another week, I had no excuse, and I gave in to my best friend's request to set me up on a blind date with a guy named Jon Mueller for a New Year's Eve party. I had one condition. I would go out with him if we had lunch at a nearby restaurant. If the date didn't work out, I could walk home.

We agreed to the daytime date, and December 31st arrived with a sense of trepidation, an unseasonably warm day. He was on time. Footsteps reverberated through the empty hallway, followed by a knock at the apartment door. Through the wooden slats, I saw a tall, handsome man wearing a leisure suit and white boots.

He said, "Is this the place where a beautiful Cuban girl lives?"

My heart melted. I opened the door speechless, and he took the opportunity to say, "I have my car outside. Ready to go?"

I nodded and said to my mom, "*Hasta luego Madre.* See you later, Mom."

A knot formed in my stomach; aware his eyes were on me as we walked toward his blue Camaro. He opened the door, and I slid in.

A gentleman! I guess I could forget about the white boots for a while.

During lunch, we talked about what we did for a living. He was a mortgage broker for Beneficial Finance, Inc. I told him I studied at the community college. We chatted about his two tours in Vietnam and the Army Special Forces reserve. I didn't know how I felt about his military background and vocation but was attracted by his confidence and maturity. He was easy on the eyes—steel blue eyes, black hair, and firm hands.

He was impressed with my knowledge of forensics and C4, an explosive compound. I imagined myself married to the man in front of me, sharing a home, lots of books on the wall, and it felt right.

He dropped me off at home, stole a kiss, and asked me for a New Year's Eve date. Dizzy with excitement, I entered the apartment, turned to Mom and Glori and said, "He asked me to go out tonight, and I have nothing to wear! What am I going to do?"

As usual, the coin purse came through. Glori and I went to Miracle Mile in Coral Gables and bought a pair of black strappy shoes. She called the Cuban clothing traveling salesman and a burgundy dress, purchased on credit, appeared neatly folded on my bed. I was Cinderella and didn't have to worry about the midnight stroke of a clock.

Mom asked me to call her from the party to let her know how things were going and if I was safe. "After all," she said, "we don't know anything about this man."

Although I called her and told her I would be home by three, we left the party after midnight, parked at the beach, and the hours slipped away.

We held hands, kissed, and talked, getting to know each other. The intense attraction was a threat to my virginity.

I returned home in the wee hours of the morning to a mom deliriously mad, thinking I had met my demise at the hands of the Americano. I apologized quietly and went to bed under a barrage of angry words.

"What were you thinking? You shouldn't put yourself in such vulnerable situations. A decent girl. What if..." On and on, she continued.

She didn't sleep that night.

I didn't either, thinking about him.

From then on, Jon and I dated and talked on the phone every day.

He was promoted to office manager the same day we met, and I continued my studies at Florida International University.

I learned he didn't believe in marriage or had a desire to have kids. I didn't press, but one evening laying in his full embrace, he professed his love to me.

That summer as part of my studies, I left to work a temporary co-op job at Dow Chemical in Midland, Michigan. It was lonely being away from each other, and our love grew through our correspondence and sometimes talking on the phone. He came to visit in July, and we celebrated our country's bicentennial birthday together.

Back in Miami, Jon told Glori he was going to propose in September, on my birthday. They crafted a story about him buying a winter coat as a gift, and when he came home to pick me up for dinner, he said, "Sue, I'm so sorry your present didn't arrive."

Turning to my sister, he enriched the tall tale, "Thanks for helping me out with the coat size. It's so disappointing it didn't get here on time."

They continued bantering back and forth, and I thought the exchange was odd but figured he had bonded with my family while I was out of town.

We drove to watch the sunset at *Los Pinitos*, the bay bottom beach on Rickenbacker Causeway on Biscayne Bay. He got out of the car, came around my side as though he was going to open the door, and said, "Can you reach into the glove compartment and get my glasses?"

"Sure," I said. Reaching in I spotted a brushed white gold diamond ring in a black velvet box.

I ran into his arms, and he said, "Well?"

"Yes!"

I married my blind date in November, eleven months after we met, and Glori and Mom assured me they would be fine.

As a cross-cultural couple, we encountered misconceptions. There were plenty of opportunities to misinterpret in-laws as we piloted through situations and the small things of everyday living inherent in each other's culture.

I encountered shades of bigotry from strangers during our first years of marriage. Once I was even asked by a superior at my workplace why Jon married me when there were so many pretty American girls. I was young and naïve and didn't know how to answer the cruel question. I carried my hurt home where Jon told me how to respond the next time a similar question came up.

He said, "You tell them that I love you because you're beautiful, sweet and smart. There is no one else I want, and I'm a lucky man."

A few years later, before we traveled to California to meet his grandmother, Jon's mom received a letter from her best friend coaching her how to break the news that I was Cuban. A friend's guarded love, or spiteful ignorance?

We started a family in 1980 and moved from Homestead to Brandon in 1984 when Jon was promoted to vice president with Beneficial Finance. Jon was tasked to develop Harbour Island, now a thriving residential island in downtown Tampa. Subsequently, he formed his own business, a profitable mortgage banking company, and I joined Tampa Electric Company as a chemist, where I worked and enjoyed an incredibly rewarding career for more than thirty years.

We grew as professionals and improved our standard of living. We raised a beautiful family, enriched with the addition of four grandchildren.

I never forgot the lesson of managing money using the beaded coin purse. It wasn't a lesson about paying my way, rent, or utilities. It was an exercise in living as a loving and nurturing family to overcome difficulties and reach success. Our move to the Tampa Bay area became an excellent transition from the South Florida bigotry, since in Tampa I passed as a second- or third-generation Cuban, or Italian.

THE ROCKING CHAIR

1989

The Rocking Chair
I don't remember the heat of summer
nor the coolness brought by the rain.
But I can still feel the strength of your oak frame
rocking me, the curve and sloping details of your armrests,
and even the little indentation where your joints met.
I'll come for you.
Soon.

   Susana Jiménez-Mueller

My childhood rocking chair became a part of my personal infrastructure when in 1959 I sank in despair as Dad pulled its rockers off and threw them on the other side of the car—a maimed chair.

The rest of her was secured in the trunk of my uncle's car with a rope circling the varnished wide oak seat and under the finely detailed arms. A rope in a series of loops around the rear bumper threatened to destroy the exposed rounded corners of the inlaid cane on her back and seat.

We left for San Felipe and a part of me lay on the ground with the rocking chair rockers, needing to be resurrected in a future time and place.

The wisdom of age and the loneliness of physical loss caught up with me as an adult. I wanted, I needed strong roots, like those of pesky weeds that can't be pulled. I desired to bring home to the United States my injured chair to make us whole.

A sense of urgency drove me to travel to Venezuela in 1988, and in my Aunt Celia's house I found my chair shoved against a wall, between more boxes, old newspapers, and magazines. I wondered if she felt abandoned like me? Slowly, I walked through the piles, inching closer to her all the while making sure I had a way to escape if any pests crossed my path. Cloth rag in hand, I dusted and moved her to the living room.

She was fragile.

Anxiously, I loosened the joints with a hammer, fighting for her life, subconsciously knowing I had to be prepared to let her die if her wooden parts broke. One by one, the pieces came apart, the arms, the back, the legs, and the seat. I stacked the pieces, wrapped her in brown paper, and tied the bundle with rope.

We came home safe, and I learned how to replace the rattan cane and refurbish the wood—all this before the advent of the Internet! Maybe someday I will have someone make her new rockers. Presently, I'm content to sit in my sixty-five-year-old chair, my link to home and a time when my family was intact.

ORPHANED AGAIN

1988-2002

The Reflection in the Mirror

Behind my door, I see you in a wakeful dream.
I shed joy but have peace.

The softness of your embrace
and the smell of Coty powder on your skin.
Pink rogue and lipstick.
Your laughter.
You loved to laugh.

Now and then, when the sun is still pale
in the morning sky, and the
bathroom light is dimmed, I see your
reflection in mine.

Your soft, worn black comb now in my
hands, glides through thinning hair – a
road well-travelled before.

The hand extends, fingertips barely
touching the cold mirror.
Its hardness softens, and I reach you
through the void that separates us and
know I am an extract of you.

Inspecting the face, neck, and hair, I
hear the echo of your words in a
whisper, "When did THIS Happen?"

The reflection dissolves.
Yet again, it is me.
A faint smile crosses my face.
I shrug and brush my teeth.
Susana Jiménez-Mueller

I never had time to grieve for my dad at ten, my sister, Glori, at twenty-three, or my mom at forty-eight. Life's problems got in the way. My spirit was in a state of flux, as far back as I could remember, and I was thirsty for stability and a break from loss. I was tired of straddling two cultures.

Since moving to Brandon and settling into rewarding careers and a family life, my spirit began to heal, and I didn't have to rely on resilience to get me through to the next hour or the next day.

Mom had moved to Brandon from Miami to be near us and help with the grandkids. We were happy.

In the late '80s, I started to notice almost imperceptible changes in Mom's personality. She started liking tomato soup and salmon cakes, enjoyed playing vinyl music records, had very little patience with

154

people, and her social filters became thin. She said what was on her mind—it wasn't always very nice. This, of course, didn't occur if she was around her two grandchildren, Rebeca and Zachary. She pronounced his name with a soft *S*, Sakary. They were her little princess and prince, her *niñitos*, little children.

Mom started painting her nails red and wore a couple of inexpensive rings on her fingers.

She would say while contemplating her hands, one hand gently resting on the palm of the other in front of her, "I wear these rings so people's eyes will be drawn to them and not see my wrinkled fingers."

Maybe this was not as much the result of the disease, but a coping mechanism. She was old and didn't like it... but who does?

The changes became more pronounced by the time she was ninety-one, and then at ninety-two, she was diagnosed with Alzheimer's, and the precipitous mental and physical decline occurred.

One day during lunch at her apartment, I showed her a picture taken in Venezuela when I was nine years old, and Glori was twenty-one. She recognized her daughters but argued that I was not her "Susanita." My heart broke in a million pieces, and I felt abandoned and desolate.

I was an orphan again.

How can Mom not recognize me?

I couldn't shake the feeling of emptiness, loss, and sorrow. Once again, I entered into resilience mode.

Caring for her took more and more time. I visited her for lunch every day, and although she didn't remember me anymore, she always recognized her grandchildren. I was just the kind lady who helped her each day. I adapted to the new situation and took solace in knowing I could still enjoy her company, learning to love her in new ways.

We laughed a lot.

She died one month after reaching her ninety-three winters, and I began to think back on all those earlier Alzheimer's pivoting, branching points on the tree of her life. I remembered how she gave nicknames to certain things she didn't recognize by their common name. For instance, take radishes, the small, round, vibrant, spicy red vegetables with a white heart. Mom called them *besitos* because they reminded her of kisses. While grocery shopping, I also referred to them the same way, and before long, I forgot their real name, too!

I think it was April 2002, three months after she had passed away, when Jon and I sat in the back porch of our Brandon home as he listened to my reminiscing. In silence, we watched squirrels chase each other as they hopped from limb to limb. The squirrels would stop short enough to twitch their tail and snap their heads up and down as if saluting each other before they began the chase again. Chasing each other? Chasing the wind? Marking their territory? I didn't know and didn't care. It was very relaxing to watch their antics, and for a moment, my mind leaped to thoughts of radishes and pointing to the squirrels in the tall, freshly clad green oaks, I said, "Jon, look at those radishes!"

Since then, jokingly, we refer to squirrels as radishes and are tickled studying their eating habits. In January, all the oak trees shed their leaves, and radishes scurry around our backyard to find nuts. They settle on their favorite rock to crack them open and eat the soft melon-colored flesh, tails always twitching. As I work in my garden, I'm reminded of my mother when I see the remains of these meals. Not because she particularly liked squirrels, but because our word associations created a memory that lives in me and brings me joy.

Perhaps finding joy in life is like trying to find water in a desert. It requires focus and time to reflect on the microscopic to find connections with our environment and those around us.

Now, I take pictures of squirrels during my travels because it makes me happy. I have pictures of squirrels in Yosemite, California, and in Glacier Park, Montana. With their thick and fluffy coats, those radishes don't resemble their Florida cousins, but their tails twitch all the same.

We recount this story to our children and grandchildren to remind them it is just a game, and in the future if they hear us calling squirrels *radishes*, don't think we have gone over the deep end.

DON'T WORRY MOM

2001-2019

My Boy

Behind my door, the heavy heart learns
to bury the words we can't face.
I can't protect my boy.
Blood of my blood,
life of my life,
I pray to God—no more war,
as air draws from my lungs.

Tic toc, tic toc.
Time passes.
The sun rises,
day after day.

Boys have secrets.
Men make pacts.
Boys play with toys.
Men face facts.

Old war—new war,
it's all the same.
Seasoned soldier, new soldier,
protect yourself and stay sane.

Tears swell, and
the heart beats.
Keep walking—just breathe.

I could hear his voice whispering
in my ear, "Don't worry, Mom."
                    Susana Jiménez-Mueller

My soul was raw. The following years would prove to be some of the hardest years of our lives.

The death of my mother was followed by ceremonies, graduations, and weddings for our children, Rebeca and Zachary, and then Zachary joined the Army.

We were empty nesters.

By the summer of 2003, Zachary and his wife, both soldiers in the Army, were in Iraq as part of Operation Iraqi Freedom.

Before he left, I gave him a journal to track his days and help him find refuge from hell. In the journal, I wrote to him and shared my childhood memories.

I had no escape.

For Christmas, we wanted to send him a taste of home, and Rebeca and I made him grandma Maxine's fudge, except it turned into hard candy - he loved it anyway. During his deployment, I worked and kept myself busy organizing my mother-in-law's eightieth birthday party and a family reunion for my maternal side of the family, Los Rodriguez - Cardenas y Perez - Sarduy.

Jon and I lived like shadows until the spring of 2004 when they came home after nine months of deployment. At the airport, Zack and I held tight in a quivering embrace, a flashback of when I held him on my chest, minutes old.

Happiness flooded our days upon their return, and we prepared for Maxine's birthday celebration. We held the party in her backyard, which felt like a one-hundred-and-eighteen-degree oven surrounded by cacti, misters, and Hawaiian music. In the rear, a scraggly roasted pig with a green apple under its chin lay on the table as a centerpiece under the huge grapefruit tree. This was June in Phoenix, Arizona.

Rebeca danced the hula for her grandmother while Zachary and Rebeca's husband, danced behind her, smoking cigars, coconut bras over white t-shirts tied at their bellies, and grass skirts, a la World War II movies where soldiers entertained each other. Tiki torches threatened to set the boys' hair on fire. How magnificent to see all three of them dancing! For a brief moment, Jon and I held hands, leaned on each other, and our spirits soared like eagles climbing higher and higher.

There were three additional deployments to Iraq for Zack, a total of forty-eight months. We sent care packages with cookies, gloves to hold the hot gun, and a small pillow to cradle his tired head.

I never knew of the conversations father and son had before each deployment. Ten years later, I stumbled upon information about the stealthy exchange, face to face, sharing agony, and conversations about death.

Jon, also a war veteran, had said to his son, "Don't let them capture you alive. Go down fighting. That is the only way."

The discussion was necessary, as Jon later explained to me since the Taliban's way is to videotape the beheading of soldiers to instill dread.

After each deployment, Zachary shared the journals with me, except for the last one, where he made a note of an IED explosion and how he ran blinded by the concussion until someone stopped him. The blast, ameliorated by a metal sign, almost took his life. Back home, he shared the incident with his sister and said not to tell us because we would worry. But how could she not? Our family had no secrets, and now he was suffering from a concussion. Relieved he was home; all I could do was cry.

My spiritual journey was marked by a profound sense of being connected to my creator. But at times during those years, I couldn't even pray to say, "God, you know what we need."

Instead, I found comfort praying a rosary, a distant memory from my childhood, living with my godparents in Venezuela.

I got used to talking to God during the day, lifting prayers for our children, their families, and us. At night, I surrendered to the rosary and sleep while nine hours ahead, my son was fighting. During the day, I believed he was safe in deep slumber.

We carried sadness and worry, anger and pride. It seemed an unusual combination of feelings. We feared our son would return with emotional and physical wounds.

Zachary had chosen a military career.

Whenever I stand at attention reciting the Pledge of Allegiance at an event, my eyes fill with tears of gratitude for the country that adopted me. And full of love for my parents, who made the hard decisions and sacrifices to bring us to America. Undeniably, I wonder if they ever contemplated having a grandson fighting for this land, now my land—our comingled Cuban blood at the ready.

As a family, would we ever be called upon to pay the ultimate price for freedom?

Our children and their families are doing well, and Jon and I try not to hold our breath in expectation of what may come next. We are poised for the rebound as a strong military family.

Somehow, we endure and continue to bend in the wind, seeking peace.

WIND AND WATER

2012

Wind and Water
I roll over for air and see four ibis
flying overhead in perfect formation.
How did they learn to feel the air
around them and ride the wind?

I roll over and my hands enter the water.

Slowly exhaling, palms open, digging deep in the water.
Going slowly, I swim faster.

Like the Ibis, I fly free.
  Susana Jiménez-Mueller

I grew up sheltered from some normal kid's activities. Sure, I played jacks, cards, drew, colored, and played with dolls. I even sewed. But I didn't roller-skate, ride a bike, or participate in sports, outside of the school curriculum. Specifically, I didn't swim.

Many times, people asked, "How come you can't swim? Weren't you born on an island?"

I always responded, "We lived far from the ocean."

What I really wanted to say was, "After my father died in New Jersey, and without insurance, my mother was scared I would break a bone or worse yet, be in a terrible accident and die. I wasn't allowed to take any physical risks on land or water."

Mom told me repeatedly of her responsibility to keep me healthy and safe so I could grow up and live out my dreams she and Dad had sacrificed so much to make a reality.

And so, I missed out being a kid.

Sometimes I attempted activities despite being scared something would happen to me. How could I face her if I got hurt? I needed to be responsible.

The lack of basic kid skills affected me in later years, when as a young woman, I couldn't join in most fun activities with friends.

After Jon and I married, I taught myself how to roller skate and ride a bike. Swimming though, remained an ongoing issue. We lived in a second-floor condominium in Hialeah, Florida, near Miami. Early one Saturday morning, my stomach flipped as I stepped into the open breezeway on my way to the laundry room. The sunlight reflecting off the pool's surface, the openness of the hallway, and the drop from the second floor to the pool overwhelmed me. I slammed my back against the wall, closed my eyes, and shuffled along until I felt the edge of the door to the laundry room and entered its safe hold.

In the laundry room, my feet held fast to the floor like the anchors of a ship and kept me in place as I swayed in waves of nausea. Blood rushed cold through my veins, and my throat tightened. I couldn't breathe. I leaned on the closest washing machine until my heart stopped pounding.

I loaded the washing machine and planned how to return to the condo. I would face the wall and inch my way back to the building. I recognized I had a fear of water, pools, and heights.

Jon never knew of that incident until years later.

Sometimes, we went to the beach for a weekend, and he swam or jet skied. I stayed out of the water occupying myself with walking and collecting seashells. Each time I had an excuse not to enter the water and carried a burden, feeling inferior to others at the beach and poolside.

We planned a trip to Sanibel Island, Florida, and Jon made reservations at a quaint resort. I decided to surprise him by learning how to swim in one week—an outrageous goal for me.

My swim classes were in the evening at a pool managed by the YMCA. During the first class, the instructor told me to close my eyes, hold my breath, and float on my front in waist deep water. I floated, overjoyed.

During the third session, I floated and decided to open my eyes, and I lost it. I LOST IT! The bottom of the pool was DOWN THERE, and I was UP HERE. I didn't return to class. Jon and I went to Sanibel, and I collected more seashells.

Meanwhile, our little family grew, and we moved to Central Florida and had one child ready for swim lessons. Armed with courage, I took our daughter Rebeca to swim class and endured cold sweats, witnessing our toddler struggle in the water.

She told me with trembling lips, "The water is cold Mommy."

My heart sank, but I remained resolute for her and for me.

Rebeca learned to swim in no time and by then Zack could wear a toddler life vest. I passed the time standing in the pool with them, afraid a kid would bump into me, and I would "fall" to the bottom of the pool.

I decided to try swimming classes again and enrolled in another adult swim class. I discovered goggles, and now I could see the bottom of the pool. Most of the time I stood paralyzed in front of a very real-feeling wall between the water and me. Feet planted firmly at the bottom of the pool, legs shaking, I couldn't let myself go and float. I remained embarrassed and frustrated.

Occasionally in class, I pushed myself to maneuver into a front float. I used a kick-board, always afraid I would lose the grip and fall. Every awful experience increased my fear. After a few summers of classes and repeated frustration, one weekend Jon and I went to the pool with the kids.

Daringly, I called out to him, "Hey, watch me!"

I succeeded in swimming about five feet to the wall in four feet of water and panicked when a gaggle of children swam under and around me.

I didn't return to the pool.

When the kids were older, we took the family to Negril, Jamaica for Fourth of July weekend. The warm water, a splash of color ranging from aqua to cerulean relaxed me. The creamy sand and picturesque boats interlaced with the aromas of Caribbean food and salty air held me in a trance.

Every day, early in the morning, we walked down the footpath to the beach, returning to the bungalow late in the evening. On the trip,

I learned to use a snorkel in one foot of water, advancing to snorkeling in four feet. I played in the water with the kids all day long!

At the end of the weekend, we were waiting for the bus to take us to the airport, and I waded back in the water fully dressed. I'm sure it looked peculiar to the people managing the hotel. Rebeca joined me unconcerned. I wanted the moment to last.

Back home and with renewed hope, I anticipated finding a solution to my problem. This time I opted for hypnotherapy. During one of the sessions, I regressed to the age of six months. In the regression, I recalled Dad, Mom, and I were visiting a house with a broad, deep, square water well.

In Mom's arms, I heard him say, "Honey, please be careful and hold the baby tight, so she doesn't fall in."

This memory, released in therapy, focused on yet another set of details to my already extensive list of water and height hazards. Did I imagine this event, or did it really happen? I couldn't be sure, regardless, my brain believed the memory.

The hypnotherapist taught me a progressive relaxation exercise with directions to execute it every night. It consisted of imagining myself in a full scuba suit, a la Jacques Cousteau, entering the ocean at a beach. Slowly entering the surf and walking deeper and deeper, looking around and watching the fish. I attempted the exercise and pulled myself out of the visualization feeling my throat closing. I stopped the progressive relaxation exercises but continued the hypnotherapy sessions, still hopeful.

In the winter months, in addition to the hypnotherapy sessions, I self-prescribed visits to a local gym with a small warm, shallow therapy pool. The indoor pool bathed in a yellow light created an ambiance of tranquility. Every day after work, I floated alone in the pool. Every day the same. I pushed off the side of the pool and floated in the heavily chlorinated water until I reached the other side, nearly three feet away.

Summer arrived again, and I enrolled in what I trusted was my last swim class. To no avail, the result remained the same. I still hadn't realized the common thread between the encouraging Jamaica experience and the therapy pool—warm water! Hypnotherapy had only helped me understand the roots of the fear, not heal it. Resigned, I declared myself an aquaphobic and was done with classes.

Twenty-seven years later, after many attempts to learn to swim, the method to heal my fear of water and begin to heal the fear of heights literally fell in my lap.

Late spring of 2004, Rebeca brought home a St. Pete Times article about adults learning to swim. Melon Dash, the developer of the Miracle Swimming for Adults Afraid in Water (MSA) system had just concluded teaching a class in Safety Harbor across the bay from me.

I saved the article and told my daughter I had come to terms with being aquaphobic and was done with trying to learn to swim.

Before my fiftieth birthday I found the article hidden under papers, discussed it with Jon, and enrolled in the five-day MSA class in Orlando. Proving that for me, giving up hadn't been an alternative.

After completing the first MSA week-long class, I visited the pool almost every day to desensitize myself and obliterate the fear of water. Although every visit wasn't perfect, I never pushed through a skill because I understood chasing the skill would only make me nervous. My goal was to be calm to swim.

I logged over one hundred visits to the pool and took additional classes, first becoming free in five feet of water, then nine, until the depth of the water wasn't a concern.

The transformation took a couple of years, one day at a time.

I sat underwater smiling with internal joy as I recognized I could help others by teaching and mentoring.

My swim journey included becoming a water aerobics instructor, and an MSA swim instructor, helping others overcome and heal their fear of water. I taught my first swim class in Safety Harbor, the same place showcased in the newspaper clipping!

I kept a journal to document my transformation and to someday share the message with the world because I knew no one had to live with a fear of water. Using the journal, I wrote and published *Now I Swim,* and as of this year, I've been swimming for sixteen summers.

STEEL-TOE BOOTS

1985-2018

A Salute

To the women and men
who have shared the early
mornings and nights
supporting the restoration of light.

And to the women and men
who have made me think hard
and try harder than ever
to bring a sense of right.
I bow to you.

Three, four, and six days,
we've shared the laughter until we cried
about stories of people
near and far.

2004 it is not!
But why would it be?
Hurricane Irma certainly was not a
Charlie, Frances, or Jeanne.

Under the cloak of planning,
a new temporary logistics unit came to be.
Pillows, cots, and towels,
propane tanks—mass management,
and other things.

Watching you track the
movement of trucks and supplies,
as easy as it may seem,
sent a chill of pride through me.

Seventeen years of planning,
seventeen-hour days.
People, laundry, meals, busing,
lodging, rain, and wind
topped with a tragedy
in our midst.

Hurricanes Irma, Katrina, Stan,
Wilma, Frances, Charley, and Jeanne
gave me new friends, not just colleagues.
A farewell it may be, but know that I
will always remember the small
moments,
and thank you. Believe you, me.
Susana Jiménez-Mueller

As a chemist, I saw myself conducting research, not bench work. Wearing a clean, crisp white lab coat and stylish safety glasses, lab book and black ink pen in hand, I documented research, solving problems, finding a new substance that could make daily life easier for the world.

In the daydream, the air flowed through my fingers as I picked up a pipette, with the low soothing hum of the nuclear magnetic resonance equipment in the background. I worked alone and loved it. Clean glassware stood like soldiers along the top tier of the work bench, some tall, crested with thin lines and a pouting lip, a graduated cylinder, others fat and round with a long neck, the volumetric flasks, waiting for instructions. A gray scale sat among spatulas and wax paper on a separate table. At the far end of the room, the glass hood safely held concentrated chemicals and fuming acids. My lab had a large window overlooking a deep green pond. There were seasons and the tree's changing colors, as well as the geese, told me of the passing time.

It was a beautiful dream.

When I joined the Tampa Electric Company Causeway Laboratory in December of 1985, my blue jeans and blouse were protected with a white lab coat. Three of us tested coal, ash, and oils, and made a great team—probably the best in tune team I had ever been part of. In fact, anyone observing us work the calorimeters, ash fusion furnace, and scales saw a well-choreographed dance. Three chemists transitioning, pivoting, rotating, and analyzing. We took turns prepping coal samples and, in those days, we looked like miners with coal dust covering us from head to toe; the lab coats might as well have been black. I hated prepping coal samples but enjoyed troubleshooting instruments.

A year-and-a-half passed, and a position came open in the environmental department. I applied, and soon after that, I transferred downtown. The casual dress was swapped for a business-like suit and high heels. The new opportunity still brought days of jeans, this time paired with steel-toe boots, safety glasses, and a hard hat. Field days included overseeing underground and above-ground storage tank removals, developing environmental programs, inspecting solid waste and hazardous waste contracts, responding to down pole-mount and pad-mount transformers in the early hours of the morning, fires at substations, hydraulic or mineral oil spills, and environmental compliance audits.

Once, on our way to audit a waste disposer incinerator, I flew in a Leer jet over Tennessee and sat in the copilot seat. We sliced the clouds and glided on the carpet of white for a while. Then the airstrip below peeked through the billowing vapors, an indication we would land soon. The swift descent was a surprise. The wheels touched the ground, and the plane rocked from side to side. Just like that, we landed.

Different audits took us into Alabama and other states. On a particular trip we got lost driving in the middle of swampy nowhere. We stopped at a restaurant and ate flaky deep-fried freshwater fish crusted with cornmeal, grits, and green beans as sides.

For thirteen years, my environmental job was to help protect water and land, always keen to work projects where I could use chemistry to solve environmental challenges. I even planted fields of sunflowers and used bugs to eat a diesel spill. A lot of my time was dedicated to reading and interpreting regulations, the least exciting part of the job. By the end of my assignment in the department, I had the opportunity to lead the compliance team and the stewardship program, which included the Manatee Viewing Center, in Apollo Beach.

Developing guidelines, programs, and writing plans placed me at a great advantage to observe, learn about the company, and glean how each department worked to support the generation, transmission, and distribution of electricity during storm events. I learned that when bad weather hits, many employees are needed to orchestrate an exemplary level of response and recovery. It occurred to me that staff are the company lifeblood and essential not just to response, but also recovery.

Developing the first Environmental Storm Response Plan and a vision of how to use the Incident Command System during storm response and recovery catapulted me into the next seventeen years of my career. I developed and implemented an Emergency Management and Business Continuity Program for Tampa Electric and TECO Energy, Inc.

A "whole community" approach to preparedness was necessary to ensure skills were paired with emergency response and recovery jobs to support operations. Slowly over the first seven years, the grassroots effort to teach and promote preparedness culminated in an employee base which strongly embraced personal and family preparedness and their emergency job assignments.

Every storm and event allowed us to tweak the plans as part of a three-legged stool approach—employee-company-community preparedness. Employee preparedness became a crucial aspect of resilience in a changing world after the attack of the Twin Towers on 9-11.

I would be remiss if I didn't note that the exposure to the MSA swim system in August of 2004 served to keep me centered as I managed over five hundred logistics employees during the response to the back-to-back hurricanes that same year, hurricanes Charley, Frances, and Jeanne. The following hurricane season saw me managing the response to TECO Transport remotely from Tampa when Hurricane Katrina decimated their operations, leaving twenty-three feet of water in the office building and fish caught in chain link fences. Hurricane Wilma, later in the 2005 season, hit the Miami area, and for the first time, I supported Peoples Gas in their restoration.

There were many other storms and national events where an all-hazard approach in preparedness served us, as well as the community, supporting local and federal preparedness to bring best practices and also help the electricity industry. I sustained a vision of holistic preparedness as my education expanded to support my assignment, earning certifications in Maritime Security, Emergency Management, Physical Security, and a master in Business Continuity Management.

I wrote the poem at the beginning of this story on September 13, 2017, the third night of our response to Hurricane Irma. It's a tribute to the men and women who worked alongside me and helped build a culture of preparedness at TECO Energy. Notably, a shout out to my team along the years—Sue Connell, Angie Leslie, Audrey Cain, and Kelly Knigge.

I was blessed and very fortunate to retire on April 1, 2018, as the TECO Energy, Emergency Management and Business Continuity Director with an over thirty-two-year career full of challenges, opportunities, and growth.

Sometimes our dreams become a reality taking a different shape. I didn't have a full career as a chemist, nor did I find a new substance that would make daily life easier for the world, but my chemistry led me to a legacy which will make a difference in the Tampa community as well as the electricity sector for years to come.

And who knows, maybe I'll still find a new substance in the form of a cookie to bring sweetness to many lives.

DANCING A JIG

2018-2019

Dancing a Jig
I'm made of mountain fog
and the sugar cane juice that runs
through my veins like sap.

I'm the whisper of far-away languages
and the women that came before me.
I am their essence, you see.

I'm midnight serenades,
guitars, harps, and castanets.
I'm the coolness of the early
morning breeze.

I'm made of green pastures, mountains,
snow, and slow-moving rivers.
I'm made of long white linen dresses,
lace, and parasols for sunshine and rain.

I'm made of deserts, valleys, and bucolic places.
I'm the woman under a thatch roof,
dancing a jig.
    Susana Jiménez-Mueller

My verbal and written Spanish skills waivered in my tweens as I favored communicating in English, the result of an early language assimilation. Culturally lost, I adapted to exile in Miami while submerged in a recollection of Cuba, in the shadow of my mom, family, and friend's memories.

Mom imbued me with a love of Cuba I could only taste through her memories, poems, food, dances like *la jota*, the jig, and the *mazurka*, a popular Polish dance in the 1920s she danced with her mom and sisters and later with us. I've taught my children and grandchildren.

She became the axis I rotated on, as well as the star which I revolved around.

In front and center was an unshakeable faith in God as she spoke of the need to *hacer familia,* to nurture family, unite people. I learned about our family and the past from anecdotes and stories about war and spies and the lives of our ancestors in Spain, the Canary Islands, and Cuba.

I heard the same stories whenever a memory stirred in her or when she became lonesome for her homeland and a large extended family. I was amazed she remembered so much when nothing was written. The stories intrigued me, and I wanted to understand how their lives intertwined on an island, a distance of ninety miles, yet emotionally a million miles away from me.

Although names like Espinosa, Cardenas, Jiménez, Rodríguez del Rey, Perez de Morales, Lopez, and Sarduy became part of my personal infrastructure and story, I had an insignificant understanding of the people they represented and asked myself where I fit in the sea of names.

Due to different circumstances and my sister's poor health, we moved between Venezuela and the United States four times. Each time we carried less and less, but each time Mom made room for our picture box. It contained diplomas, birth certificates, pictures, as well as small mementos authenticating lives lived.

As a teen in Venezuela, my heritage didn't serve as a passport to enter the inner circle of school friends, and in Miami I straddled cultures outside the Cuban influenced neighborhoods. Becoming a naturalized citizen at twenty years of age were words on a paper, signed and stamped by a judge. Although the document indicated the United States had adopted me, it would take years before I felt American.

I wasn't the only young Cuban-born asking, "Where do I belong, and what is my identity?"

I knew I came from Spanish stock. I was born in the Caribbean. I struggled with not having a patch of soil and felt I couldn't call Cuba nor America my own.

Through genealogy research I learned of Jon's family's military service heritage, which provided a rich perspective on what it meant to be an American. I grew roots sharing a life with my husband and seeing his love of country. Through him, our children, and my work, I became part of the American fabric.

It wasn't until commercial DNA testing and genetic genealogy that my search culminated in an explosion of findings on my own tree. I found distant cousins on the same quest for identity and roots. Yes, I validated the European ancestry which was not just Spanish but included Portuguese, French, Italian, Irish, and British, with some Eastern European, Jewish and Native American. I was blown away by this last finding. My ancestral maternal clan's footprint is in North and Central America and the Andes. I can only assume one of my ancestral mothers was brought to Cuba to augment the labor force as part of the Spanish conquest of the Americas.

My ancestral mothers had been here for thousands of years. Amazing! My sense of not belonging to a tangible patch of soil dissolved instantly.

I expanded my understanding of self, in the context of genetics, in the stories my mother told, and in the new family connections I made with distant cousins as we each traveled our genealogy journey together. Aside from estimating how long ago my Native American ancestral mother lived in Cuba, I also found my European family made Cuba their home since colonial times.

To close the ancestry loop, I visited the city of my birth in 2019. Our daughter Rebeca and I arrived in Santa Clara, Cuba, on Sunday, May 12th, Mother's Day. How perfect to have her with me as we celebrated the day as moms and embarked on a ten-day adventure to meet distant cousins for the first time and familiarize ourselves with the city and the island.

On Sunday, Cousin Melinda picked us up at the airport with a driver and an *Almendron*, an old American car. After effusive hellos, the bags were stuffed in the trunk and ourselves in the cushy back seat, without seat belts—those were never available in 1950s cars. We rambled through the outskirts of Santa Clara to drop off the luggage at the bed and breakfast and pick-up Isabel, the owner and possibly my cousin, on our way to Cousin Norma's for Mother's Day dinner.

The car turned the corner, and there was Norma, five years my senior, and her entire family waiting for us outside. The car stopped, I opened the door and sprinted to her. The first indication I was among family was embracing Norma's fragile figure, as she exclaimed, "*Oh, como si estuviera abrazando a Tía Marta, gordita.* Oh, it's like hugging Aunt Marta, a little chubby." Endearingly, Norma was referring to Mom and her middle-age spread.

We sat in Norma's living room. Relatives stood at the open door and leaned in through the window smoking and listening to stories. Talking about our lives and the situation in Cuba became the ice-breaker. Teens also sat listening without electronics to call their attention. Mid-evening, Isabel took out a picture of her aunt Ñica, and I inhaled a gasp. The lady in the photo was identical to my paternal grandmother, Vicenta!

I exclaimed, "Oh, My Lord, Isabel. I think this picture validates the hunch we are related."

We arrived at Isabel's house a little after midnight and sat around the dining room table drinking coffee. I waited as she pulled out family notes from a spiral bound notebook. On the upper right-hand corner, in black ink, I spotted my great grandfather's name, Vicente Espinosa Cardenas, jotted almost as an afterthought. His name written sideways alongside her great grandmother's name, Mariana, indicated they were siblings.

I buzzed. I found a connection to my paternal line.

There wasn't a day I didn't meet a relative, from the person who helped us exchange euros for convertible pesos in a busy street corner to the driver who took us on fantastic excursions to places like Trinidad, Cayo Santa Maria, and Hanabanilla.

On Tuesday, Rebeca and I set out to Trinidad, a world heritage site, on our first adventure with Norma, Melinda, and Jonas. It was a party on wheels with the lush green of the *campo,* countryside, framing the wild groves of tall Royal Palms. We rode with our windows open to the wind and the coolness of the Sierra Maestra mountain range where Fidel Castro had made his enclave sixty-four years before.

The long car trip in the Almendron and lunch at La Marinera restaurant were perfect settings to get to know each other, often cramming years of family information in short exchanges. If I took a moment of silence for myself, I could hear several conversations transpiring at the same time.

I said hugging Norma laughing, "You talk more than I do!" Everyone joined in mirth.

In Trinidad, we visited a museum located in a former affluent colonial home—*The Museum of Architecture*—walked the cobbled streets, shared a taste of a *canchánchara,* a mixed drink made with *agua ardiente* (the first distillate from sugar cane), lime juice, and honey, at the Taberna la Canchánchara. I danced with Melinda to live music, with on-looking, Russian tourists.

The conversation on the return trip to Santa Clara was only diverted by snapping pictures of horse drawn carts, *guajiros,* cowboys on horseback, and stopping at a roadside stand to buy mamey, Melinda's favorite fruit.

On Friday, the last of the rain drops vaporized from the sidewalk adding to the heaviness of another breezeless hot day. We arrived at Norma's late morning and Percida, her daughter, lent us, flip flops, and we too spilled out onto the sidewalk. The young cousins smoked short cigars while Melinda and I discussed a hand drawn family tree using the window sill as a counter. The movement between Percida and Norma's homes was fluid as refreshments were served.

In the living room I set up a makeshift interview area using the antique oak sofa as a side desk and sat in a rocking chair, two fans moving the warm air.

Melinda made cancháncharas with ice cubes. Cuban crackers and mayonnaise were presented on a small table, to which I added a small bag of roasted almonds. The almonds were a hit, each person took one nut and nibbled slowly savoring its saltiness. I wished I had more almonds to share.

I continued to partake of the offerings, drinking the concoction, setting up my portable scanner and digital recorder. Soon, Norma brought a small white envelope with pictures. She sat alongside the digital recorder and handed me a one-hundred-fifty-year-old photograph of my great grandfather Sebastian and her grandfather José, my grandfather's brother.

I recognized the picture as soon as I held it in my hands. Years ago, I was given a copy of a document written by a descendant of Great Uncle Máximo, José's and Manuel's sibling, which mentioned the picture. The paper also stated that no one knew who had the photograph. How fortuitous to have stumbled on the photo and its owner!

I examined every detail. The sepia picture was mounted on black cardboard with scratches and holes. On the back, the writing in pencil was undiscernible. I grew concerned the photograph would not fit in the portable scanner, but it did. Meanwhile, our recorded conversations were tracking the momentous occasion. Trembling, I took the picture in my hands. I should have worn white gloves.

Other pictures came out of the envelope, each as precious as the last.

On Sunday, while visiting Rosa, Uncle José's daughter, we were surprised to learn Numidia, her sister who lives in the States, had reminded her to show us *la casa de lo abuelos*, our grandparent's house.

Abuelo Manuel Rodriguez Cardenas sold the Manajanabo *finca*, his farm, in the 1930s and moved to Santa Clara with Abuela Eleuteria, and the girls, Marta (my mother), Celia, and Adela who were in their twenties.

The 1850 colonial house they rented sits on Máximo Gomez between Julio Ober "San Vicente" y Marti. The house doesn't have a number but sports an UNEAC sign. It's a gathering place for writers and artists, *La Unión de Escritores y Artistas de Cuba*, The Union of Writers and Artists of Cuba (UNEAC).

These homes were built in the form of an *L* with the kitchen and dining room at the back of the house at the base. The living room was the space located as you entered through the front door. To your left was the first bedroom, the only bedroom with a window. The rest of the bedrooms were situated along the breezeway, and somewhere in the center, a bathroom with toilet, sink, and bathtub. After the Cuban Revolution, the house was merged with the house next door by demolishing the wall separating the courtyards.

La casa de los abuelos looks brand new, retaining the original hand painted blue tiles with pink and yellow roses in what was the living room area. I don't know if the exterior and interior walls were painted as they are now.

As you exit the house, to your right, up the hill, you can get a glimpse of *El Parque Leóncio Vidal*, the central park. We couldn't help but notice that in those days Mom only had to walk a few blocks to the *Ayuntamiento,* City Hall, where she worked as a clerk.

Thanks to Juan, also an author, Rosa's husband, we gained access to the house, and Rebeca took videos.

Our flexible schedule and outlook proved to be a plus since the trip itinerary I had carefully shaped in past months changed completely to accommodate plenty of family time, excursions, and genealogical surprises.

Visiting the house where my mother met my father was amazing. With old pictures, I transported myself to a time and place where her future still shone brightly and then remembered her last day when she, due to Alzheimer's, became restless, and wanted to go home to her parents and siblings.

I asked myself: Where is home? What is home? Is home a state of mind or of the heart? Is it the home of your parents or the home where you raised your family?

I understood maybe it's all of it, bundled, slipping in and out of time.

For fifty years, the Hudson River area between New Jersey and New York City pulled at me with memories of the last place where our family was whole and where my father took his last breath. I was ten years old. It still feels like home.

The trip to Santa Clara, the city of my birth, sealed my identity and gave me closure. Battling and trying to fit in with one culture or the other ended, and that gave me room to fall in love with the Spanish language.

Finding lost family connections, photographs, homes of old, and piecing together my identity as a Cuban-American required patience, perseverance, and resilience. Genealogy provided the tool and coping mechanism as I dealt with change in new environments. My faith in God and the love of my family supplied a framework to accept my identity.

Blossoming as a Cuban-American was like finding water in a desert. My thirst for belonging and assimilation drove me to reinvent myself time and time again as I adapted. Thanks to God, family, and the people who inspired me throughout life, I can say I'm no longer culturally lost. I've reconciled my identity.

I'm the woman under a thatch roof, dancing a jig.

EPILOGUE

For me, the success of the collaboration effort became a realization because we each brought our best skills to the front and center, allowing everyone space to tell their story.

The process validated our stories as we experienced how different four women with Hispanic roots can be - from the way we tell our stories, to our personal voices and beliefs.

Most importantly it reinforced our desire to showcase our individuality and carry the message that no-one should dictate success boundaries to others. We each stand in our uniqueness, like our fingerprint or DNAprint. As humans we have the capability to succeed and have a happy life – on our own terms.

IN APPRECIATION

I offer my undying love and gratitude to my parents, Orlando and Martina (Marta), who taught me perseverance, work ethic, and a love of God.

My sister Gloria who was like a second mom and a wonderful sister.

My mom and Jon, my husband, for their support as I embarked on different projects throughout my life.

My daughter, Rebeca, and son, Zachary, for always providing solutions and input. I so enjoy the adults you have become!

My family, Los Rodriguez, too many to name, for being our safety net and a beautiful example of what being a family is about. Cousin Manolito and his wife Edith, Lidia and Damaris, Ricardo, and Nora for supporting our Rodriguez genealogy research. As well as My DNA cousins, instrumental in finding genealogy gems along the way: Loly, Carilyn, Osmi, all the Marias, Viccky, and Reinaldo.

Elsie and Ernie Rodríguez, my childhood friends, for making me feel I was like any other kid.

Maria Rey, Angie Leslie, Jamie Woodlee, Pat Boody and Stephanie Kilborn for being part of my TECO family and my friends through thick and thin. Vilma Brueggemeyer and Maggie Dominguez for being my mentors. Albert Perotti, Jr. for opening new opportunities in the world of physical security, and being a friend.

Spence Autry, a friend and co-writer, for introducing me to Val and to the Bloomingdale Writers Connection.

Our grandkids Xavier, Logan, Raiden, and Brandt, for teaching me how to be a kid again.

My thanks to Val Perry for introducing me to Life Story Writing. Parts of this anthology have roots in the Bloomingdale Writers Connection life story classes.

Last but not least, the co-authors of this book, for their dedication to our project, and becoming my island sisters.

Figure 6 – Santa Clara, Cuba. December 1959 - Susana...and her present-day rocking chair without the rockers.

Figure 7 – Caracas, Venezuela. January 1964 - L to R Sitting: Tío Pedro, Mom, me, and Dad. Glori is standing behind the bench.

REWRITING

Jean Morciglio, Ph.D.

PROLOGUE

Sand and Water

I remember little from my earliest childhood, mostly snippets, images and feelings - a few actual events.

I do remember being held underwater.

When my mother retells this story, she thinks I was two, maybe two-and-a-half years old. We were having lunch on a crowded beach. My mother hadn't grown up near beaches—she grew up in the snow and rain. She set me in the water with the hope I'd play with the other kids.

A girl next to me, not much older, stood up, walked over, and smiled at me. She reached down and pushed me onto my back until I was under the water. I didn't feel scared, but I had a toddler's sense of right and wrong: I knew she shouldn't be doing it. Only, I couldn't move. I opened my eyes and saw her through the water, wavering above me.

She wore a striped red and white bathing suit with a black flounce skirt and the sun sprayed behind her head and shoulders. She kept her hand pressed on my chest. It was a pretty day. I laid still, watching the girl smile at me.

My mother says she doesn't know how long it took before she noticed I wasn't sitting up in the water anymore. Eventually, she appeared over the girl's shoulder, pulled at the girl, then yanked me from the water.

When she re-tells this story over the years, she sometimes adds, "What kind of kid doesn't cry?" I wondered about that myself. Later, though, I decided that if I had cried or struggled, I might have swallowed water.

Sometimes, knowing when to breathe and when not to breathe underwater is important.

LATINX-*Mix*

What do you do when you're ten years old and your mother still tries to set you up on play dates? My immediate plan of action was to scare the poor girl. So, Cindy and I sat at the edge of the roof on my three-story apartment building, a roof with no guard rails or safety barriers. The town of Yauco, Puerto Rico spread out below us and up the hills around us, like a half bowl. I let my legs dangle over the small lip on the edge of the roof to make Cindy a little more nervous.

Although almost four years older than me, she pulled her knees to her chest with her chin pressed on top of them, as though making herself smaller would prevent her from rolling off. Her blond hair, pin-curled into wavelets, unraveled in the wind. She wore shorts and a blouse tied in a knot above her stomach. I wore a cutesy matching short set my mother picked out, like I was six years old. I kicked a piece of tar off the side of the roof.

I'd learned about the rooftop getaway from David and Murray, two boys living in my apartment complex. We climbed up to the roof often to hold mock sword battles with broom handles and sticks. It was a place no adults visited. The boys were older than me, but I tagged around after them any time they let me. We hiked through the sugarcane fields and along deserted canals. We climbed the densely vegetated hills that surrounded the town. My mother called me tomboy then invited Cindy over.

Cindy's mother and mine met at an army base fundraiser and hit it off. My mother went to the bases often, not just to promote our hotel, but because she met other women who spoke English, enjoyed playing cards, and making hats. She never felt comfortable attempting to speak Spanish, although our family had lived in Puerto Rico for several years now. She hadn't made many friends with the locals.

Cindy described herself as an "army brat" when I walked to her house and picked her up after school. She would spend Friday night and Saturday with us at the hotel. Her family moved all the time, she droned on, especially to "countries" that were being developed, like Puerto Rico. Didn't she know Puerto Rico was part of the United States? I'd detoured on the way home and bought some comic books at the local *bodega,* drugstore.

"Where are you from?" she asked. I always found that question hard to answer. We had lived in Flint, Michigan, when I was younger, but we'd been living in Puerto Rico for a while, and it seemed our permanent home. My mother, brother, and sister were born in Flint. My father, me, and a twin brother who died shortly after birth, had been born in Puerto Rico.

At the end of World War II, Angelo Juan Morciglio, from Yauco, Puerto Rico returned from the war a captain with a bronze medal, purple heart, and lots of front-line action. He opened a small restaurant in New York City. Lottie Shaheen, daughter of Christian immigrants fleeing religious persecution in Lebanon, pleaded with her parents in Flint to escape her role in the family grocery business. She left to study fashion and design in New York. They met, fell in love, and decided to marry. Her parents were against her marrying a Puerto Rican. His parents, Puerto Rican landowners of Italian heritage, didn't want him to marry a non-Puerto Rican. So they eloped. I loved that story and thought them very brave. I grew up traveling between Michigan and Puerto Rico.

We spoke only English at home. My father used his inherited family beachfront land to build a hotel, the *Mar y Sol,* in Guánica the next city over. On weekends and during the summers we lived in the hotel because my parents managed it. We lived in Yauco. We lived in Guánica. We lived in Flint. I didn't know how to answer her.

"Look at the size of that house," I pointed, ignoring her question and forcing her to look up. In the hills to the left, beyond the endless sugarcane fields that waved and dipped in the sun, a few gigantic mansions and plantations popped out above the greenery. The growers and other wealthy families lived up there, surrounded by fenced areas for horses, farm animals, and outbuildings. Then I pointed to the right, to the town. To the opposite types of homes on hill sides; tiny and stacked together.

"Hey, there's my house," she said, singling out the roof of the house her family was renting, about five blocks away halfway between the two extremes. Non-native families and middle-class Puerto Ricans lived near my apartment complex. Most lived in Spanish colonial-style homes, two story, open-air, concrete buildings, the cars parked at the ground level, and living quarters on the second story to catch cool breezes.

Beyond the mid-sized homes, you could see the plaza and church, surrounded by a few blocks of shops, then more housing that tapered off into smaller and smaller households. The houses climbed up the sides of the hills that encircled Yauco. At night the hills blinked with the lights of the families that lived there. *Jíbaro*. Hill people.

"And my school," she pointed to another building a few blocks away.

"Where do *you* go to school?" she turned and looked at me as though it finally occurred to her we didn't go to the same school. She, David, Murray, and most of the other English-speaking kids around us attended Island Preparatory Academy.

As though on cue, we heard David and Murray climbing up the metal rungs that led to the roof. I ignored them, thinking they might sneak up behind us and give Cindy a pretend shove to scare her, as they often did to me, to see if I would flinch. Instead, they seemed happy and sat down next to her, one on each side. They attended the same school, although she was two years ahead of them.

They pointed out some of the sights I had just shown her, but she listened as though it was new and interesting. David pointed to one of the ranches above the sugarcane fields. He told Cindy about how we had hiked there, and they convinced me to sit on a rickety fence and throw rocks at a bull to see who could run away the fastest. When it charged, I was last to get away. I rolled my eyes and flipped through the stack of comic books I'd brought, ignoring them. They weren't helping me scare off Cindy.

Most residents in this apartment building were from other places around the world. David's father was an engineer from England. Murray—or Muddy, as we called him because that's what it sounded like when his mother called for him—was from Scotland, his father an architect.

"I go to *Santo Rosario,* Holy Rosary, next to the church," I interrupted them, after the boys pointed out their school again. It sat next to the town's main church and faced onto the plaza. Cindy squinted.

"We wear the green jumpers and white blouses," I said, thinking of what might make the most sense to her. Each school in Yauco, public, private, or Catholic, had its own uniform. In the mornings you could see kids walking through the plaza, heading in different directions. Girls at Cindy's school wore tan and blue plaid skirts and tan blazers with a crest-shaped emblem on the lapel. The public school girls wore pale navy skirts and white blouses.

Cindy nodded. She knew the green jumpers the Catholic school girls wore.

"But how do you speak Spanish?" she asked, pointing to my Spanish comic book, *Archie y Veronica.*

"How do you *not* speak it?" If you live somewhere, learn the language, I thought.

My classes were in Spanish. We learned about being *Boricuen,* Puerto Rican. If I didn't learn Spanish, I wouldn't know what was going on. I had become the interpreter for my mother, the person she sent to the post office for stamps or to the drugstore for cigarettes. And I became an interpreter for kids at school who asked me to write notes for their English-speaking friends. My father was proud of me. At school, we were preparing for the annual Christmas pageant, and the play would be in both Spanish and English. Since I was good at both, they'd asked me to be the narrator.

I was friends with many local girls, had dinner with their families, but my mother still insisted on introducing me to the daughters of women she met on the army base. This was her third attempt, and I was getting good at scaring them away.

We heard a horn honk below.

"We're going to the hotel," I said, taunting David and Murray. They loved it when we took them to the hotel, and they could spend the day on the beach or the pool. Now I wanted to punish them, they seemed so awestruck by Cindy.

We led her back over the metal rungs down to a patio, then down the stairs to the second floor and rear balcony of my apartment. As we entered, we could smell frying *empanadas,* meat pies stuffed with beef and olives. Martita, our maid, not much older than Cindy, stood in the kitchen door. She helped my mother with cooking and cleaning. She smiled generously and slipped us each an empanada as we passed.

My older sister, Chris, sixteen, joined us as we headed downstairs to where my father had loaded our belongings into the Jeep. I pulled a pomegranate from a bush in front of the building and gave it to Cindy, but the look on her face suggested she didn't know what to do with it, so I dropped it in the food bag. I knew if I gave her enough challenges, she would not come back.

Chris, Cindy, and I piled into the back of my father's Jeep. I loved riding in the open air in the back of the Jeep, holding on to the braces, and feeling the air on my face. My sister hated it because it messed up her hair. I figured Cindy would, too. My mother and a little brother took a *público,* a public car that traveled between main stops in each town, so they could do some shopping on the way.

Getting to the Mar y Sol, in the next town, Guánica, involved a drive over mountainous back roads, near cliffs, and through curving hairpin turns. Then suddenly the ocean stretched out for miles, turquoise and beautiful. On bad weather days, rare on this part of the island, my father honked the horn entering every blind curve, reminding the drivers coming from the other way not to veer into our lane. When the road was being built, my father talked about meeting with many road commissioners and planners, taking them out to dinner, getting to know their families. It was the way business happened, my father explained to me.

We pulled up to the hotel and bellhops ran to help us unload the car. I led Cindy through an open-air walkway towards our rooms, but when we passed the formal dining room, she stopped, pulling on my arm, pointing.

I thought she was looking at the bronze life-size statue of a pirate holding his cup to the sun. My father had commissioned it for the hotel landscape because his ancestors had been privateers who helped the queen of Spain, the story went. Two brothers who came from Italy, probably Corsica, were then ceded land in Guánica, the land my father eventually built into the Mar y Sol Hotel. It was also rumored that Cofresi, the Robin Hood pirate of the Caribbean, had buried a treasure near our land. I loved the stories of ancestors and pirates and treasures.

But that's not what Cindy was pointing at. She was pointing at a framed picture of a newspaper article on the wall.

"Is this where you met her?" Cindy asked, referring to the story on the wall about Marisol, and I finally understood why she had agreed to hang out with me, a ten-year-old. I thought back to the day the picture was taken.

I loved the lifeforms at the edge of the ocean and spent hours collecting them. One day I found empty cigar boxes in the trash bins behind the restaurant. Perfect display boxes. I placed ocean objects in each box, then lined them up on both sides of the six sloping stairs leading up to the hotel's formal dining room entrance. I exhibited starfish, sea urchin shells, mixes of coral, crab skeletons, a dead sea cucumber, even odd-shaped pieces of petrified wood. I couldn't wait to show my father.

The sound of a helicopter landing on the beach brought everyone running out of the hotel. My father showed up to greet the helicopter, but not alone—he had a crowd behind him, reporters with blue flashbulb cameras, suited men looking unlikely on a beach, and they gathered around a young woman getting off the helicopter.

Marisol, a famous island actress, ducked down, walking below the spinning blades. Laughing and waving at everyone, she followed my father to the entrance of the hotel, up to the dining room steps. The group stopped, and she patted down her blond hair for the photographers. My father, in his best suite, took a place at the top of the steps. Then he noticed the open cigar boxes on the steps. He whispered something to the restaurant manager, Charlie, standing just below him.

I could tell he wasn't happy.

Charlie was nice. He made me a fried shrimp dinner or a frozen guava drink whenever I asked for it, even though they weren't on the menu. He shook his head, and I realized he might be in trouble. Inching my way through the crowd up to my father's side, I whispered, "They're from the ocean," feeling this explained why the boxes belonged there. My father gave me a long look. It might have been the wrong thing to do, or at least the wrong day to do it, I thought.

Instead of saying anything, he pulled me into the crowd and moved me to the step next to Marisol. She leaned down and put her arms around me without looking, her smile facing forward for the cameras, her caked-on makeup face next to mine. Light bulbs flashed, and shutters clicked. The next day I would see our picture on the front page of the local paper, Marisol's arms around me.

The crowd of reporters continued shouting questions at her, then they all surged around me as she followed my father into the dining room for the rest of the press conference. I stayed on the steps guarding my treasures, not old enough to know what was important in the world. Someone had framed that newspaper article, and it now hung on the wall outside the dining room. Cindy must have seen a copy of it before today.

"What was she like, up close?" She stopped to study the picture.

When I didn't answer she added, "I want to be like her."

I once again ignored her and headed straight to my family's living space. They always reserved Room 1 for the owner's family, a large suite for my parents and little brother with an adjoining bedroom, where Cindy, my sister and I, or any friends we brought along, would stay during the weekends.

Living in a hotel as the owner's daughter is a little like being a

Disney princess. Someone makes your beds every day. Your room is always clean. They make the meals you ask for in the restaurant. Everyone, from the wait staff to the maids, finds you a delightful person. I might have developed an unrealistic view of my place in the world.

That night we ate dinner in the open-air dining room facing the beach, while my sister began telling irritating stories about me.

"She thinks she's a mermaid," she started in, telling my least favorite story.

I loved the ocean. I swam and collected interesting objects I found in or along the water's edge. The beach sand was white, the water was turquoise, clear and clean as far as the eye could see. Saltwater never bothered me. The ocean was full of life. Sea birds circled and called above, always searching. The sand rippled, almost alive, with the imprints from waves and the bubbles left from tiny hermit crabs, exposed as the waves receded.

Often, I made friends with kids staying at the hotel. Once I met a boy and a girl from the States who dabbled at the water's edge. We played together and made sandcastles for a while. I produced a pile of interesting objects for decorations I had found under water—broken sea urchins and glossy shards of shell.

I heard them whispering, and I could tell they were talking about me. I was becoming irritated when they finally asked me the question that was bothering them: how long could I hold my breath under water? I explained that I didn't hold my breath.

For some reason they didn't believe me. We argued about this for some time, and I was hurt, so I showed them. I dove under water, picked up shells, followed fish, and played around, relaxing and breathing the whole time. When I surfaced, instead of agreeing with me, they acted more confused. I was bossy enough to think about kicking them off of what I considered *my* beach.

Shortly, though, an older girl and already a teen and a stand-in for my mother, came down the beach. She joined the group and after hearing the discussion, and both sides of the argument, she resolved it for everyone. I was a stupid child, she explained, and human beings absolutely could not breathe under water.

I still hold this against her. After that day, I couldn't breathe under water anymore, and began to measure my time there.

My mother brought up an even worse story.

The previous November we'd eaten in the formal dining room instead of the more casual open-air restaurant because of the stormy weather. David, Murray, and their families were with us. The sky held grey with clouds; the palms leaned sideways, pressed by the wind, and the usually calm waves came in over five feet high. I noticed David and Murray sneaking out, so I followed them down to the beach. They taught me a new game on the edge of the water—bodysurfing.

As the waves receded from the shoreline, we ran out after them. We sat down and curled into a ball. We caught a ride back when the new waves would hit, then roll us, head-over-heels, somersaulting to the shoreline. When the water caught me, I just relaxed. I even opened my eyes and saw the water and sand spinning round me and felt the joy of being propelled through the water at a high speed, tumbling all the way.

My father and mother have always been very different in their parenting styles. My mother had a short fuse, and if you set it off, she would smack you with a hairbrush, a coat hanger, or whatever was handy. My father was the opposite. He rarely raised his voice. He let you know what he expected of you, and if you didn't meet his expectations, he had a way of looking at you, and you knew you were doing something wrong. If he looked disappointed in me, I might burst into tears.

That day, though, I heard my father yelling. Running to the beach, waving at us, shouting for us to come out of the water. He grabbed me then shooed us all away. David and Murray's parents were right behind him. They lectured us to stay inside and away from rough waves.

"What kind of kid…?" my mother said to Cindy, who'd looked impressed until my mother began telling her about things *not* to do during a hurricane.

After the body surfing incident, I started to have a re-occurring dream. I had it again that night, sharing a double bed with Cindy in the hotel room.

A woman steps out of the ocean, as tall as a three-story building. She isn't from the ocean. She is *the ocean.*

She has driftwood-colored hair that hangs down her back. It's tangled like dreadlocks, with shells and seaweed caught up in the strands. Her skin is the color of sand. She wears long, shredded shorts and a tattered white t-shirt. She is muscular, fierce, and self-contained.

When she wants to, she comes to the water's edge and walks along the coast. The shoreline heaves and rolls where she steps. She ignores me, just as she ignores everything on the beach. She doesn't care whether you are a human or a crab. If her walking disrupts any creature or crushes anything, hotel, house, or natural landscape, it makes no difference to her.

When she walks, all life must respect her, not the other way around.

I woke up on Saturday morning sweating from the dream.

After dressing in swimsuits, we grabbed juice and bread from the outdoor restaurant, then headed for the pool. I tried to show off by doing somersaults off the diving board as Eddie, the lifeguard, taught me. I was working on a two-and-a-half. I considered Eddie my friend, since I spent most of my weekends on the beach or in the pool, and maybe my parents considered him my babysitter. But because Cindy said she didn't swim well he spent the day showing her strokes instead of noticing my flips. I was ticked off about being ignored. When we drove back to Yauco on Saturday evening, dropping Cindy at her family's home, everyone smiled and invited her back except me. Then we went back to our apartment to sleep.

We got up early as usual on Sunday morning, and my father went out to buy a newspaper and a fresh loaf of *pan de agua,* a long baguette with a thick crust, we ate with melted butter and fresh fruit for breakfast. I dressed for church but took my book, *Heidi,* down to a patch of ground behind our apartments. The flowers smelt fragrant in the crisp morning air. Later, when we all assembled to walk to church, my mother stared at me.

"What's *wrong* with you? Your hair is a mess. Your clothes are dirty. You have been lying under that tree reading, haven't you?" She held me by the shoulder as she brushed off my clothing. She and my sister looked immaculate, every hair in place. I looked at her with no understanding. I couldn't imagine how anyone would value looking good over reading a good book.

We walked to the plaza as a family, strolled around a few times, saying hello to many of the families seated on benches or walking, then headed into church for Sunday Mass. Santo Rosario church was beautiful, outside and inside. I stared down at the tiled floors and made up games in my head, like imagining patterns in the ornate tiles and thinking up stories about how they had been made that way. A statue of Mary glowed with innate goodness while a long-suffering Christ hung from a cross as a reminder of his sacrifice.

Many of the older, more traditional women flapped ornate fans to keep cool and signal their friends. They wore *mantillas*, large triangle lace scarves in ivory or black, to cover their heads and shoulders. My mother stuffed my book in her purse after she noticed me trying to open it.

I spotted Raquel, a friend from school. I ran over to her as soon as Mass was over, and she invited me to her home. I begged, saying we needed to practice for the Christmas pageant. Anything so I would not be put up with Cindy again.

I felt like I was between a rock and hard place. Raquel was the top student in our class, got the highest grades, and was good at every subject. Bone thin, she tied her curly reddish-brown hair back at the nape of her neck, and she wore the same handmade, hand-embroidered pink dress she wore every Sunday. She and I had one agreement, a secret pact. We had vowed to each other that when we grew up, we would be nuns. But lately I had not enjoyed playing with her at all. I was restless and preferred hiking with the older boys.

After some debate, my parents agreed I could go to her house for dinner.

As we walked to her home with her family, I told her about Cindy, then realized Raquel had been to my apartment many times but never to our hotel.

"Why don't you come with us? We can go swimming."

She laughed at me.

"My mother would never let me go alone. My whole family would have to come," she explained, and I pictured her and her four sisters fitting in the back of our Jeep.

"We'd all have to get bathing suits, too," she added as if she knew what I might say next. We walked through back alleys and up narrow cement stairs that led to her home up the side of the hill. As we climbed higher, the road disappeared, and we had to take the steps to reach the houses. Water ran down gullies next to us as we climbed up rows of steps past tightly packed houses painted brilliant colors—magenta, neon lime, and bright pink. As we climbed higher, the concrete homes gave way to smaller and smaller tin and wooden homes, still painted with bright colors.

Her house was mid-way up the hill, wooden, painted a bright blue, with one white trimmed window. It consisted of a front room and two small bedrooms with a walkway to the back patio. It was always immaculately clean. The front room held a wooden table surrounded by several chairs, a crocheted rug, and a pole lamp next to a green vinyl couch. The kitchen was part of the walkway to the backyard, one side containing a small stove, then a sink above curtained shelves that held pots and pans, next to it a white refrigerator. I had watched several men carry that refrigerator up the hillside steps to the house since no cars could come this far. Plants, much taller than me, filled the yard that climbed up the hill and stretched out to merge with the neighbor's gardens. Laundry flapped in the breeze. Chickens and roosters crowed continuously as they pecked and scrambled freely through the garden.

I followed Raquel into the bedroom she shared with her sisters. When she opened her own small cupboard to get out a box of mashed up Barbie-type dolls, I noticed only one green uniform and one other dress besides what she had on. She wore a clean, crisp uniform to school every day, so it had never occurred to me to wonder what was in her closet.

Her mother made a tray of *budín de pan*, raisin bread pudding, which she served with dollops of canned cream for lunch. Sometimes on Sundays she made *flan*, egg custard with a syrup of caramelized sugar. I envied Raquel for having a mother who was home, made food from scratch, and spent her free time laughing with her daughters. My mother was so busy helping run the hotel.

We sat on the rug in the front room and played with the Barbies, designing outfits by tearing off sheets of toilet paper from a roll her mother had given us, wrapping them around the dolls in complicated ways and walking them down make believe runways. After we played, I ate a dinner with them, *mofongo*, mashed stuffed plantains, thanked them, then headed down the hill before dark.

I liked Raquel, but the dolls were getting boring to me. They were too babyish. I wasn't a child anymore. But if older girls were like Cindy, I didn't want to be like her, either. I wanted to be like Heidi. Brave. I wanted to be like David and Murray. Explorers. Even if they led me to places that weren't safe, like the bull corral, or into strong waves, or up to a rooftop. Especially if they did.

Just a few blocks from home, I stopped at a corner of the plaza near a man pushing a small metal cart and bought a shaved ice, drenched with tamarind syrup.

"Give my respects to your father," the man said, handing me my cone and some change.

Sunday nights were usually spent quietly getting ready for school, but my mother stopped me when I walked in the door.

"Last night your dad asked why you don't help him with his boots anymore," she stated. When younger, it had been my job when my father came home late and tired to help him take off his work boots, to unlace them and pull them off his feet while he sat on the couch and drank a glass of water. I didn't think he'd noticed I'd stopped.

Didn't anyone know I was now ten? I didn't want people telling stories about me at dinner. I didn't want to play with dolls. I didn't want to be set up with play dates. I didn't want to help with boots. I was too old for all of it.

I stormed off to my room to read.

Later that night, I was in the front room when my father came home from the hotel, and I planned to ignore him. He walked in wearing khaki pants, a white t-shirt, and work boots, which meant he had been doing physical labor, like helping with landscaping, instead of his typical managerial duties. I might help with the boots, I thought, since he looked tired.

He walked in and leaned up against the wall. My mother handed him a glass of water, then I watched it slip from his hands and shatter into pieces on the ground, as he held his hand to his chest. He crumpled and slid to the floor.

My mother screamed for me to go to the house down the street and get the doctor who lived there. Her panic scared me more than anything. I ran, as fast as I could, down the stairs of our apartment building, through an alley, to the gate of the doctor's home, and up a flight of stairs to their door. I knocked and knocked and knocked and waited. But no one came. I knocked some more.

I gave up and ran back to our apartment. Now the lights were on in many other apartments. People crowded around our doorway so I couldn't see inside, but I could hear my mother wailing. When I tried to get in, Murray's father put his hand against my chest to stop me.

"You'd better not go in there," he said. His wife came and took me and my brother to their apartment.

My father was 46 years old when he died. I would never see him again.

Immediately after my father's death, everything spun like a tornado. They put together a funeral in just a few days. My mother asked me if I would stay home and watch my younger brother instead of going and I agreed, not realizing until later that my entire class would be there, as well as hundreds of people from Yauco and Guánica. I wouldn't see my classmates, my teachers, or my friends again, either.

My mother's brother showed up, packed us up, and within a few days whisked us to Flint where the rest of my mother's family lived. We were living in my father's world and my mother never felt right there. Now she just wanted to be back home. When we got to Flint, they sent us kids to stay with my *Sito,* my Syrian grandmother, because my mother had a "nervous breakdown." They admitted her to a hospital, and she stayed there for the next few months.

Sito spoke only Arabic, and came to America with her husband and son. We'd grown up hearing stories of them hiding in caves in the mountains, Christians fleeing religious persecution. She emigrated long before my mother was born, coming to Flint because of a strong Greek Orthodox community. She and *Jido,* my grandfather, opened a butcher shop that eventually became a grocery store. Their oldest son became a doctor.

They built a large double-sided house, the store, and an apartment building on Saginaw Street, Flint's main road, where we stayed while my mother was "ill." The tan, double sided Victorian home with neat brown trim was surrounded by plants and flowers. Upstanding, it was the focal point of the street. When I was younger, we'd lived in that house for a while, in a neighborhood with Italian, Jewish, Polish, and other families living in the apartments nearby.

I remember when I was little, sitting next to Sito on the couch and playing with her hands.

"Where did you get this tattoo?" I'd asked, as I pulled at the skin on her arm. According to my sister, they were forced to get the tattoos because they were Christians. I would pull up the skin on the back of her hand and it appeared to pull away from the bone creating rivulets that looked like lava pouring down a mountainside, and I was fascinated by the texture. She allowed this invasion patiently.

She converted spools of thin ivory-colored cotton thread into lace. The intricate, off-white creations covered every window, table, chair, and dresser in her home. She baked daily, shaping small balls of dough, then flattening them out on wooden half sphere. Next she placed the dough in a fiercely hot oven until an air pocket popped and it toasted to a light brown. The finished pita bread was eaten hot, sometimes drizzled with butter.

She wore black lace shoes with short, thick heels and opaque flesh-colored hosiery held up by rolling them just above the knees. Her uniform was a black dress with small white polka-a-dots. I remember playing in her closet once and being amazed to find many similar dresses, neatly ironed and hung—I had assumed she wore the same one every day. She often covered the dress with a white apron, the type butchers use, not Betty Crocker, using the corners to dry her hands. She kept her hair in a long silver braid rolled in a bun at the back of her neck. When she looked at me, she tilted her head slightly to the right with a smile on her face, and I knew that meant she loved me. She didn't speak English, but I believed I understood what she was saying. They baptized me in both the Greek Orthodox church and the Catholic church; she took us to lengthy church services held in Greek on Sundays.

I missed my father. I worried about my mother. I couldn't speak to my grandmother. I became very quiet. The sky was always gray in Flint. It was cold and snowy. I think of that time as a reverse *Wizard of Oz*. A tornado blew me from a happy, technicolor world into one that was gray and white and lonely.

After a while, my mother recovered and we moved to a tiny matchbox house on Seneca Street in a suburb on the west side of Flint. They sent me to a local Catholic middle school—St. Andrews. It didn't go well for the rest of 5th grade.

K o. Mo. Es. Tey. You. Sted." I stared at the black-garbed nun, my new homeroom teacher.

"Ko. Mo. Es. Tey. *You.* Sted," she repeated, more loudly. I couldn't think of how to respond.

"She doesn't speak Spanish," she announced to the class.

I finally understood she was trying to greet me in Spanish, ¿*Como está usted?* and introduce me to my new class at the same time. I had the urge to tell her *she* was the one who didn't speak Spanish, but I kept quiet and found an empty seat in the back of the room. Everyone looked in my direction as though I came from another planet. English was my first language. I had lived in Flint before. I didn't have any language problems.

"Why do you talk with an accent?" a boy asked me at recess.

"I don't talk with an accent. *You* talk with an accent." I responded. *Where did he get off talking to me like that?*

Still, I had a hard time getting my bearings. Nothing seemed to make sense. Before and after school, the girls all hung around together in clumps. Sometimes a few girls would come and talk to me, but when they did, they'd ask a few questions then walk away. A particular girl, Trudy, seemed troubled by me. She often looked at me with a strange expression. One day she brought a group of girls over.

"You're a spic," she informed me, as though this was something, I needed to learn about myself.

I didn't respond because I had no idea what a "spic" was. I went home and asked my older sister. It shocked me to learn not everyone thought Puerto Rican's were the bravest and the most intelligent people in the world. I was also surprised people thought of me as Puerto Rican, because most of the Puerto Ricans I'd known hadn't considered me a local, they'd thought of me as an international.

During my first few months at St. Andrews, as I tried to talk to a few girls in class, I began to think they were crazy. All they did was talk about boys, as though boys were the most interesting thing in the world, as though they were more important than girls. Which they weren't, because most of them couldn't even keep up with science class, covering subjects I had already studied.

In Puerto Rico, we held dances every Friday afternoon at school and learned steps for the *merengue* and *pachanga*. I learned appropriate dance manners and danced with boys. I didn't like or dislike them; they were just other people. I could not figure out why every girl I talked to discussed boys all the time, or why the boys and girls stayed completely separated.

My school in Puerto Rico was stronger academically, so I whizzed through my classwork, a little bored. I loved science and started talking to other kids who did, too. We all grouped together in one corner during science class. One boy, Greg, seemed to do well, and was interested in something I found fascinating—the stars. We talked about class, walking home after school a few times. He headed toward the wealthy homes north of the school. I lived about twelve city blocks in the opposite direction. I thought I had finally met someone who liked science as much as I did. Someone I could talk to.

The next day during recess several girls came up and asked me about him.

"Do you like Greg?"

I knew kids like this. If I said no, they might take it as an opening to gossip behind his back. Saying something bad could hurt a kid. So, I said yes to stop them from saying anything rude about him.

Later, at lunchtime, kids taunted him, telling him I "liked" him. Someone drew a crude picture of two figures kissing, labeled it with our names, and hung it in the cloakroom. I felt embarrassed and humiliated. I didn't think of him that way, well, really never thought of anyone that way.

He wouldn't talk to me after that.

I tried to stay away from that group of girls, but sometimes they would come up and surround me. Trudy often led the pack.

"What are you wearing to Judy's sleepover?" They'd talk about a birthday party or a sleepover that everyone was going to, apparently to let me know I was the only one who hadn't been invited. *No one has taught them how to be polite.* I held down my anger.

Another time they circled me and Trudy said, "We know you stole Stephen's pen."

Later that day, boys confronted me as well, all demanding their pens back. One boy pushed against my chest.

"What are you talking about?" I said, furious I was being blamed for their stupid pens.

I pushed back hard, almost knocking him over, and shoved between two boys to get out of the pack. *These kids have no manners at all. I'm tired of their bad behavior.*

After that I spoke to almost no one.

The nuns liked me. I was quiet, got my work right, did well on tests, and never tried to speak Spanish. My classes were much easier than they had been in Puerto Rico, but we no longer studied Europe, China, USSR, South America, Africa, or Puerto Rico. Only the mainland United States.

It felt as though the entire world was disappearing.

At home, my family seemed to be disappearing, too, losing its connectivity, everyone going in different directions. My mother started working evenings at a department store, my sister was in high school, not much interested in any of us, and my little brother was sent to a local public elementary school instead of the Catholic school.

I read more and more. My favorite book at the time was *The Witch of Blackbird Pond*, about a young girl from a Caribbean Island whose parents died, so she was forced to live in Massachusetts with her Puritan aunt. She was different, so they accused her of being a witch. I felt the same way.

I no longer had friends of any kind.

We had relatives. We spent time on weekends and holidays with my mother's family. They considered me Syrian and ignored my father's influence, never mentioning him, never mentioning his death, as though he never existed. When I visited, we ate *kibbee* and grape leaves, pita bread, and hummus. We talked about the silly things the old-timers did and our Syrian roots, although we were mostly second and third generation Flint. There were parties where people danced the old way, *dubkee,* and I learned about the music, food, and customs. Many of them were very well off, and I sometimes got the feeling I was the poor cousin they were required to be around.

My mother tried to act lighthearted, but at night she seemed so sad. Her family acted as though she was paying for her lack of good judgement, as though being a single parent was something she chose. She told a story about how she had forgotten to send in the last life insurance payment, so there was no insurance. She simply let go of the hotel, walked away from it, not fighting for the compensation owed her.

We tumbled slowly into poverty.

She was the same about parenting—overwhelmed by it, and not very interested. On most days, I tried to take care of her, make the food, watch my brother, and keep the house in shape. I thought it was my responsibility to make sure my mother didn't lose it and walk away, get "sick" again and leave us.

It was a long walk to school; I got frostbite, twice, from wearing the wrong boots, "You'll lose your toes next time," the doctor admonished me. I caught colds. Kids rarely talked to me, other than a small group of science kids. I was careful not to act interested in being friends with any of the boys outside of class.

I made one friend when our class got in trouble for talking. Sister Donahue assigned us to write an essay and bring it back signed by both parents. She dressed down anyone who hadn't followed the instructions. When she got to me, she made me stand up.

"Your father hasn't signed this," she declared to the class.

"It's hard for him. He's dead," I pointed out, hoping she could understand the challenge.

She told me to sit down. Later, she called on Janet. Janet gave the same response but more boldly, with an attitude. Sister Donahue turned red and was a little more careful about what she said after that.

In the hallway, between classes, Janet and I looked at each other and became instant friends. She was one of the few girls at St. Andrews to invite me to her home. I couldn't invite kids over because I couldn't have friends over unless my mother was home, and my mother was rarely home. Janet lived far away in a much nicer neighborhood, on the opposite side of St. Andrews. I noticed the kids rudest to me seemed to come from those nicer houses in the neighborhood on the north side of school. Many of their fathers were in management at General Motors. The families that lived near me were line workers or union stewards.

I passed the first summer on Seneca Street bored out of my mind, babysitting my brother. I had once been brave, an explorer. I had been the best in two languages. Everyone wanted to be my friend, even Eddie the lifeguard and Cindy the army brat. Now I was invisible. To my Syrian relatives I was not Puerto Rican. To the kids in school I was a spic. I didn't seem to fit anywhere. Flint was grey, cold, and wet. There was no place to explore. I missed my father. I missed my mother.

I didn't think things could get worse, but the following spring they did. Walking to and from school every day, I started to notice other kids in my neighborhood, the kids who went to the public schools. In the spring they came out on bikes. They noticed me, too.

As it warmed up, a boy named Donny sat on his bike at a corner a city block from my house. After school, when I got near, he'd start to chase me, and I'd run the rest of the way home. Just before I got to the door of my house, he would catch me, grab me, and punch me in the arm, often knocking me to the ground.

I had a permanent bruise on my upper right arm. Sometimes he would grab at my skirt and flip it up. I'd bat his hands away, usually spilling my books. My books and clothes were getting ruined in the rain and mud puddles. I started wearing shorts under my skirts every day. I would have told someone but no one was home to tell. My mother was tired when she got home late at night. I tried changing where I walked, waiting longer after school, walking behind groups of kids, but nothing stopped him.

One day, as Donny was grabbing at me in front of my house, a group of older boys on bikes slowly cruised by. Most had their hair combed back, cigarette packs showing through their front pockets, and cuffed jeans. It was still cool outside so some wore black leather jackets. They looked tougher than the boys I saw at school.

The lead boy saw Donny grab my arm. He slowed down and circled in the street in front of my house. The other boys followed him. He looked at Donny, who froze mid-punch.

"Hey, Donny," he said, continuing to ride in circles, the others following him. He looked relaxed.

"Hey, James," Donny responded, dropping my arm. I pulled free and ran up my porch steps and in the front door. Once inside I peeked through the curtains. The bikers moved on and so did Donny. But just like that, Donny never bothered me again, and I understood the boys in my neighborhood had a pecking order. Later, I would learn James also protected his mother and sister from his own father, who, too, liked to punch girls.

As I paid more attention to the bike riders in the neighborhood, I learned they hung out at a local Park, a half block away from my home. As the school year ended, I decided I wouldn't spend another summer alone, nothing to do but watch TV with my little brother, keeping the house together. I had become unknown and had almost no one my own age to talk to.

I noticed James and his pack of boys riding by my house more often. One day he rode by alone and circled, so I came out of my house and sat on the porch. He pulled in the driveway and asked me when I'd moved in.

"Do you have a bike?" he asked.

We talked for what turned into hours.

I can figure this out, I thought, though teaching myself how to ride a bike was proving harder than I expected. Pushing off one more time, I tried to keep my balance and peddle. I coasted for about ten seconds before the handlebars shimmied and I jumped off to keep from falling over.

I was twelve, and I'd convinced my mother I needed the bike to get around for the summer. My sister was in college, my little brother was at camp, and she was working. How else could I get anywhere? It didn't occur to me to ask for help learning how to ride it. It looked easy enough, but I had never been on a bike. Now, if I could just teach myself how to stay on the clunky green and white Huffy.

I heard the jangle of a bike bell and looked up to see James on his bike, hands on his high "v" handlebars, leaning back on the long banana seat. He lifted his front tire off the ground, popping a wheelie. I could tell from the grin on his face he'd been watching.

His unbuttoned shirt flapped behind him while he circled. The sleeves had been torn off for the summer heat, and a cigarette was tucked over his ear. He was tan, muscular, and with brown hair and blue eyes. As soon as they were old enough, I heard his friends would join their older brothers and sisters on motorcycles or in Dodge Chargers, but for now, they rode around the neighborhood in packs on their bikes. I wondered if I had enough courage to ride in the street rather than the sidewalk.

James and his friends, kids typically between 11 and 15, hung out together at Sarvis Park. The size of a large city block, one corner of the park held a playground with counselors and summer programs. At the opposite end was a large grove of trees that hid a grouping of picnic tables not visible to adult eyes.

The girls in the group rode modern Barbie-pink bikes, not like my green clunker, but I was determined to be one of them, anyway. I didn't go to school with them, but I wanted to ride with them.

"I'll hold it while you start." James waited while I climbed on several times and tried to get the hang of keeping a bike balanced. He never laughed. After some practice, I figured it out, and I rode, wobblily, around the block, then to the park. I followed him down a bike path to the wooded area in the park, to a grouping of graffiti-carved picnic tables pushed together in the woods. His friends were already there.

As I got to know them, I learned a lot about the other kids. Many had fathers and mothers who didn't have time for them, or who drank too much. Kids already smoking, drinking, staying out, and doing what they wanted. Hoods. They hadn't started to do real damage, yet. They'd lived in this suburb most of their lives. I was new to this territory. The boys wore jeans, black leather jackets when it was cool, white t-shirts when it was hot, and black leather boots. The girls already knew how to wear makeup.

That summer, behind those trees I learned to smoke, to swear, and sometimes drink. But mostly we just talked. They were not like any of the kids at school—they didn't have the meanness, the arrogance, the underlying cruelty.

Their lives were tough. Every day we would meet at the picnic tables in the woods, just to talk and hang out. One day Mark, James's younger brother, told us about how their father, who liked to drink, had tried to flush his mother's head down the toilet the night before until James stopped him. James showed up that day covered with bruises.

Another day Donny came to the park. He'd opened his garage doors and found his old man hanging by a rope from the rafters. That same afternoon, when he rode his bike over to tell us about it, he said his mother was too busy with the police, so she kicked him out of the house for the afternoon.

James tossed him a pack of cigarettes.

Wayne came to the park one day with buckle marks across his face and chest—he'd forgotten to do his dishes.

Craig's mother was in hiding because his father had gotten out of jail. Craig, at fourteen, was now in charge of a household of five kids,

212

cooking food for his younger brothers and sisters. He wasn't around much.

Laurie hid from her stepfather every night by sneaking out and going across the street to sleep on her aunt's couch. Her older sister was pregnant.

Through all of this they kept their cool.

As I went from twelve to thirteen in Flint, I learned there was a lot more going on in the world than I ever imagined. The kids I knew in Puerto Rico who were poor were devout, and their parents hard working. My father had encouraged me to have nothing but respect for them. These people weren't *as* poor, their houses were nicer than the one-room wooden homes, but I hadn't known adults could be so bad, so undeserving of respect. Many of the parents in my neighborhood worked on the line at General Motors, where alcoholism and drug addiction seemed to be part of the job. One girl's father was a union steward, and she was one of the kindest in the group.

I knew nothing about what it meant to be a teen. Not having friends my own age left me in the dark about certain things my mother didn't talk about. I was so naive I didn't even know what a period was until I had one. My understanding of the world seemed to pivot all at once as I heard about their lives and the realities of the world. That fall President John Kennedy was assassinated. Anger and racial violence erupted in the Flint area. I began to recognize cruelty, brutality, and death.

The Sarvis Park kids welcomed me, taught me to stay cool, and to ignore adults who didn't really care. Any adults who *were* nice usually turned out to be pervs. For the few summers I hung out with them, we avoided tangles with the law, older kids in cars, and adults determined to punish us, and held it together in the woods, usually just by talking. That group of kids riding their bikes into the woods at Sarvis Park, the ones with brutal parents and broken families, they were the people nicest to me. I could never pull off wearing the same clothing or makeup the other girls wore, and I always had a book tucked in my back pocket, but I found I could just relax with them. We sat at the picnic table behind the trees and played music—the Beatles, the Stones, and Motown on a portable radio.

I was happy I'd found a group of kids who knew about the anger, but smoothed it over, never showed it. That's what being a hood was like. They didn't take the things in life that happened to them, no matter how bad, too seriously. I learned to keep my cool, and keep my anger to myself. No one got mad or upset, no matter how bad the home situation. It was all about maintaining distance between you and those things. You are not the bad things that happen to you. You are not the adults around you. We told each other our stories, took a drag on a cigarette, and moved on. I stopped feeling so sorry for myself.

Once, while we hung out, James asked, "What's it like at a Catholic school?"

I told them that in Catholic schools, everything you did was a reflection on the nuns, the priests, the monsignor, the Pope, then ultimately on God himself, who sacrificed his only Son for your sins. You are responsible for all that if you continue to act bad. Everything, even talking in the lunchroom, is connected to your deserved guilt and the loss of your immortal soul.

"In second grade they made us go to confession every Friday," I explained. "I couldn't think of any sins because I didn't swear or talk back, and I had no clue what an impure thought was, though they talked about it all the time. Since I had nothing to confess, I figured out a plan: every week at confession I would say that I told a lie, which *was* the lie, so it met both the rules for confession and was forgiven at the same time. That's what being Catholic is like— self-criticism until you create the very thing you're supposed to avoid."

Everyone laughed at this, and I was glad to bring this small secret into the light. I didn't admit that it had once been my goal to become a nun.

"I can help you understand an impure thought," James suggested.

Later, someone produced an empty pop bottle, and we played a lazy form of "spin the bottle." The spins only counted when they pointed to the person you wanted as a partner, so you kept spinning until it did. James spun, then he and I went off behind some trees. Before this, I had never been alone with him other than sitting on my front porch talking.

I was so naïve I honestly thought he would peck me on the cheek. Instead, he slowly put his arms around me and pulled me close. I could smell his skin like sandalwood and smoke. He bent down and kissed me on the lips, long and gentle. My body tingled from head to toe.

We never did more than kiss that summer, but I finally learned what it meant to *like* someone.

As summer came to an end, I couldn't explain it, I couldn't say it, but while on the outside I tried to stay cool, I battled what was happening on the inside: I was getting angrier and angrier. I was angry at the nuns and priests who seemed to not care no matter how well I did at school. Angry at the kids in my school who were supposed to be good Catholics. They were cruel, not just to me, but to everyone who was a little different. Angry that I didn't fit neatly into any of the labels people wanted to give me. Angry at my mother. How could she completely ignore us? And angry mostly at God. If there was a God, why would he take away my father? Why would he let the kids around me have such terrible lives?

When my mother tried to take me to visit her relatives, I fought back. They didn't seem to know who I was. They acted like my father never existed and like my mother was on a lark, managing a single-parent household while working full time.

Later that summer my grandmother died.

I tried to ignore the loss. I took the anger and became quieter, like a rock. I hid everything I felt. For my mother, the losses were adding up. She had lost her older brother, her father, my twin brother, her husband, and now her mother. She became vacant and wispy, not really with us. Like *she* was being held under water.

But I wasn't a child anymore; I had friends who were experienced in the world. I didn't need and didn't care about the imperfect and uncaring adults around me. I didn't care about the mean kids at my school. Maybe I'd become the bad person that everyone at St. Andrews seemed to think I was.

After eighth grade, all the Catholic middle schools fed into five high schools. I was fourteen when I started ninth grade at St. Gabes in downtown Flint, far away from my home on the west side. Walking into that building, I couldn't help thinking back about my first week at St. Andrews. I had been so naïve. Now I could tell stories about people I knew. Stories of neglect, suicide, death, brutality, rape, incest, jail, and rage. Those stories weren't typical in Catholic schools. That first week I found my way around but couldn't figure out where to sit at lunch hour. There was no table marked *new kids who didn't belong to any cliques*, and I was just contrary enough that I didn't plan to join one.

When I lived in Puerto Rico, the local kids didn't see me as a local, while the international kids thought I *was* a local. At St. Andrews, kids saw me as a spic. With my Syrian relatives, I was only Syrian. Even with my Sarvis friends, I didn't quite fit—a book on me at all times and little skill with makeup. I quite didn't fit into any of the groups around me.

People think school uniforms are great equalizers, but they show as much about status as any other clothes. I learned all I needed from the uniforms that first week. Rich kids upgraded theirs with expensive details, watches, earrings, mother-of-pearl buttons on blouses. The cheerleaders all matched and wore their hair tied up with curled blue and white satin ribbons. The hot girls wore makeup and hairstyles from magazines, stylish sweaters, and nylons, not knee socks. Most new kids were already in groups because they went to feeder schools or churches with friends or had older siblings in the school. Trudy also ended up at St. Gabes, though she was careful not to acknowledge me in any way.

I wore a JC Penny off-the-rack navy blue box-pleated skirt, a white shirt with a peter pan collar, usually rumpled, a navy blue cardigan sweater, navy blue knee highs, and plain loafers, no pennies. My suede jacket was not quite hood rat, but almost. I sat at a table by myself at lunch, but not totally alone. I was with Isaac Asimov, reading the

Foundation trilogy.

Later that first week, before lunch I stopped in the restroom. It was filled with smoke. I didn't feel the need to smoke at school because my mother didn't care if I smoked at home. She often sent me out to buy cigarettes. Diane, a girl in my homeroom class and very popular, was the only other person in the restroom.

As I washed my hands, I noticed a pack of Kools on top of her books.

The doors to the restroom swung open and Sister Agnes, the vice principal, pushed in, waving her arms to dispel the smoke. Diane tipped the cigarette pack off her books into the sink and backed away. Sister Agnes strode over to us, glanced around the room, then finally into the sink. I was still standing closest when she pulled out the pack of Kools. She gave me a look as though figuring out who I was, scanned my wrinkled uniform and suede jacket, then narrowed her eyes. She reached for my shoulder, apparently deciding Diane didn't look like a smoker and I did.

I could have protested, but the number one rule with *my* friends was not to fink out someone else. Adults who didn't care enough to do the right thing didn't mean anything to me. Going along to her office, I missed lunch while she tried to call my mother, assigned me detention, then looked through my purse. She narrowed her eyes at me.

"I don't want any more trouble from you. I'll be watching. Three strikes and you're out. This is *strike one*," she warned as she put the cigarettes in a drawer.

I didn't respond. I couldn't care less what she thought of me. I'd learned to disrespect adults like her.

The next day at lunch, Diane saw me across the cafeteria and paused, tray in hands, then came to my table.

"Don't worry about it," I said, not looking up from my book. I hadn't done it to bond with her.

"Is that any good?" she asked, sitting down. It's the only thing she could have said that made me feel comfortable letting her sit with me.

I gave her a short version of the *Foundation* plot.

She told me she was pissed at her friends. She sat with me for the rest of the week.

Later, one of the cheerleaders, in a tangle with the same friends, came over to talk to her. Then *she* joined us for lunch every day. Heads turned. Within a few weeks I learned all the dirt on the popular kids and the cheerleaders; who snuck away with someone's boyfriend, who said what behind someone's back. The next week another girl came up and asked if she could eat with us. She said we looked like we were having fun. This was surprising because she was from one of the large Catholic families whose umpteen brothers and sisters had attended, and ran, the school. Later that month, a very prim girl, who I thought was a goody-two-shoes with all *A*'s, left her normal table and joined us, too.

We sat together and discussed the dirt about each clique without having to worry about the wrong person hearing us. With an unspoken agreement that nothing we discussed left our table, we figured out the happenings of all the different school groups.

Somehow, we were disrupting things and got looks from all tables in the cafeteria. Often, Sister Agnes came up and stood behind me as though I was a bad influence. That was an even better motivation for us. We had somehow created a neutral Swiss territory away from the cliques, stitched together a crossover group of girls, and pissed off the nuns at the same time.

Triple win. Though we returned to our own territories at the end of the day, we sat together at lunch for the rest of high school.

The 5th Avenue Grill, on the corner of Detroit Street and 5th Avenue, made up for in freedom what it lacked in cleanliness. It was the only place within a mile of our high school that wouldn't report back if we smoked during lunch hour. It's not that we smoked a lot, our lunch hour clique that had started freshman year. I didn't bother with it much anymore, and between the five of us, we shared one pack of cigarettes for the week, depending on who'd been able to afford one or stolen a pack from a parent. We just wanted the freedom to smoke if we felt like it. The Grill was busy, and no one paid attention to us. People rushed in and out, the lines to pay always backed up. There wasn't much table cleaning between customers.

We'd crammed around our usual corner table with its familiar white formica tabletop with grey metallic flecks, our red vinyl chairs with steel frames scraping on the tiled floor. A black plastic ashtray, filled with left over butts from the day's customers, sat in the middle of the table, the air hazy with smoke. We were the only people wearing the navy blue uniforms of Catholic school girls. The diner was packed with men in a hurry to get back to "the shop"—line work in the local auto factory.

The important thing was no one seemed to care we were there. When we ate in the cafeteria, a nun walked around the room, sometimes looking over our shoulders, curious about what we were discussing. As seniors we were allowed to eat lunch off campus, but most of the other seniors went to more upscale restaurants, like the food counter at Sears or Tony's Coney Island. We owned the Grill.

I wasn't much like the other girls, with my public school friends, constant reading, lack of family life, and mixed ethnicity. Somehow, I managed to get enrolled in all advanced classes, too, so I wasn't in class with most of them, but I learned so much from these girls. They taught me how to dress to look hot when I wanted to, respectable when I needed to, and how to roll up my skirt at the waist once past the initial door inspection. I, in turn, told them what J.D. Salinger was getting at, why e. e. cumming's poetry didn't need capitals, who the Prophet was, and how hobbits once carried a golden ring to save Middle Earth.

"The hell if I'm going out with him," Diane said. The star football player had asked her to the dance. "He's a friggin' cheater."

But she was expected to go with him, she knew, and it was delicate getting away without everyone talking about her. Our dating was done by social expectation. She took a drag on the one lit cigarette we were sharing.

As we talked, I reached down at the books piled on the seat next to me and did my homework for the afternoon classes, hoping to keep up my grades. The book *Dune* was on top of the pile. That I was still in school was a miracle. I just had to make it a few more weeks until the end of the year.

"So, what are *you* gonna do, Jeannie?" Diane asked. I was stressing about two boys who both asked me out for the coming Friday. I hadn't exactly said no to either, so I needed to do something.

James was the boy I "went out with" during middle school and occasionally in high school. We were on again, off again. Since we didn't go to the same school, our paths rarely crossed, and I hadn't seen him for a long time. We girls dated in packs. When one of my friends dated someone in James's group, I hung out with him. When they broke up, we all broke up. Then, when someone else got serious about a guy, we'd hang out with his friends.

When James called that week, suddenly he was serious. He had broken up with the girl he had gone out with for most of high school. We'd talked on the phone for hours, me laying on the orange shag carpeting between the family room and kitchen, twisting the extra-long phone chord in my hands, feet up on the side of the avocado green refrigerator in our kitchen.

He was a year older than me and his draft number had been picked in December. He'd gotten his call up. He knew he was headed for Vietnam. Most guys in my neighborhood didn't get deferments. We already lost several of the older boys. We sat in their front rooms and cried with their parents and sisters and brothers. Kurt just finished rebuilding his Trans-Am, I thought, as though somehow that was important.

James had gotten his dream job, working on the line for General Motors, but he'd have to give that up. Though we hadn't seen each other much during the previous year, I couldn't say no if he was headed to Vietnam. He couldn't go without someone caring for him back home, and I knew how his parents were. Drunk most of the time. We planned to go out on Friday night and talk it over. It occurred to me that there were still deferrals for fathers.

I'd already made tentative plans for Friday with David. Also a year older, he studied art at the local community college; they hadn't yet eliminated college deferrals. His family was from England and he was like a breath of fresh air. He had been a year ahead of me at St. Gabes, president of the senior class, and captain of the football team.

We met in Mrs. Love's art class when I was a junior, and again we broke the school caste system when we began dating. But we always kept it fun and dated others, too. During the last few weeks he'd gotten more serious, talked about being exclusive, even talked about a ring he was designing for me in art class.

My friends at The Grill shook their heads but offered no advice. I wanted to be with David, but it would be wrong to leave James alone. Every relationship decision seemed to be based on the Vietnam war. I wasn't in the mood to make big choices. I wanted school to be over.

"I just want to make it to the end of the year without strike three." I joked about Sister Agnes's now well-known three strike system for dealing with everyone. I had to finish this last big assignment, make it through the last few weeks, and I'd be done.

"You had the stupidest strike two," Diane stated. Strike two, she retold, happened with my older sister, who often enlisted me to help with whatever project she had going. When she worked for Arthur Murray Dance Studio, I was her at-home dance partner; I learned ballroom dancing steps (backwards). When she took literature in college, I memorized the introduction to the *Canterbury Tales* in Olde English by quizzing her. I can still recite it when I've had enough to drink.

She took college psychology and I read her textbooks, then read all the works of Sigmund Freud and Wilhelm Reich (who wrote *The Function of the Orgasm*—lovely reading for a teenaged girl) to help her write a paper. She even started taking me to her psychology class. That it took place during my Latin class didn't bother me. I hated Latin class. *Who studies a dead language?* So, once a week I skipped Latin, my last class in the morning. My sister picked me up from school and took me to sit in on her class, then brought me back after lunch. It was going fine until Trudy mentioned to my Latin teacher that every Tuesday I had a different doctor's appointment. One day Sister Agnes stopped me as I walked to my sister's car in the parking lot and asked to see my doctor's note. I was not a very clever sneak, so didn't have one.

As I sat in in her office waiting for my mother to show up, she informed me there was a stiff penalty for skipping school—expulsion. When my mother walked in, I knew it would not go well. She wore a mink stole, purchased when my father was still alive. She had on full makeup with bright red lipstick, and I realized she may have been out with someone when she got the call.

Sister Agnes asked questions about our home life. After she left, Sister Agnes shook her head and looked at me.

"Is your mother ever home?" she asked.

"She has to work. My father died." For some reason, no one had ever heard of this phenomenon and seemed to think my mother's need to work and date was a lifestyle choice. I'm not sure why, but I wanted to defend her.

"Do you even want to go to school here? There's a public school much closer to your house," Sister Agnes asked.

I had to think about that.

The cement that might have held a person in place—peers, parents, teachers who liked you—all seemed to be missing. I was working. I was making my own money. Why was I still in school at all?

But this was all I knew.

"Yes," I chose.

She gave me a month-long detention.

"This is *strike two,*" she warned me as I left her office.

I was relieved no one asked me why I was skipping school. Diane laughed as she told the story. "What kind of kid skips school to sit in on college classes?"

On the day I was due to report to detention, I just couldn't do it. I worked almost full time, paid for my own clothes and most of my own food. I had a car. My mother wasn't around much, I could come and go as I pleased. She'd stopped trying to give me a curfew. She depended on me for help with the house and with my younger brother, not the other way around. I could not sit in some room doing nothing for an hour every day for a month, not when I still had to go to work at night where they treated me like an adult. So, I didn't show up to detention. I waited to be told I wouldn't be returning to school. *Strike three.* I'm not sure why, but no one said a word.

Now I was a senior and just had to make it for the next few weeks without getting Sister Agnes's attention again. I was on the verge of trouble because I used the school bulletin board to post anti-war information I'd gotten from my sister. It was promptly pulled down, and I didn't think anyone knew it was me.

"I thought you hit strike three on our field trip," said Diane, and everyone laughed. "You deserved it, you held up our train for so long."

On our senior class trip, we took a train from Michigan to Stratford, Canada. As we got ready to cross the border, Sister Agnes walked by me and whispered, "Tell them you're an American citizen."

I nodded. *What else would I tell them? I am an American citizen.*

When the conductor came by asking questions randomly, he said, "Where were you born?"

"Santurce, Puerto Rico."

The train was held up for the next hour.

Sister Agnes was furious. "I told you to say you were an American citizen."

It took me a moment to catch on to what she was saying.

"Puerto Ricans *are* American citizens," I said.

It was her turn to look surprised. I finally understood that Sister Agnes thought of me as a foreigner.

"It's not *my* fault the person in charge of customs didn't know anything about citizenship," I said to the girls at my table, who laughed and threw french fries at me.

My last big assignment was due that afternoon. Mrs. Gordon, my psych teacher, had assigned a project where we demonstrate some psychological principle discussed in class, and I was one of the last to present. I worked out the details during lunch at The Grill. This was 1970. There were race riots in Detroit. Public high schools in Flint experienced significant racial unrest. I thought my classmates needed exposure to what was going on in the outside world. I picked out an exercise from my sister's college psychology books—replicate the conditions of an inner-city classroom.

After lunch, I stood in front of the psych class for my presentation and told them I would create a mock classroom experience. Erika was a teacher's pet, so I gave her a textbook and told her to stand in front of the class as the teacher. Anthony always bragged about planning to be a police officer. I gave him a rolled-up newspaper and told him to stand in the corner. He was the cop, but he didn't need to do anything unless there was an emergency. I gave the role of the main student to a boy who loved to show off. Then I picked out several outgoing, talkative kids and put them around him in the middle of the room. They faced Erika and stood shoulder to shoulder, just touching each other. Their instructions were to act like they were in a normal classroom, just closer together. The rest of us were observers.

Erika's job was to teach one section from a textbook and keep order.

At first everything went well, and the lesson went smoothly. Then, as the lesson got boring, one of the girls started giggling and pushed against another. As a group, the kids swayed back and forth a little. Erika tried to handle it by elevating her voice to get their attention, but the sterner she got, the more the group ignored her and talked to each other. Being so close together, they began jostling, then laughing and pushing a little harder. Following the instructions in the exercise, I got up and flicked the lights a few times.

The boy in the middle shoved to get away from the others. The kids began to push away from each other. Erika yelled at them to come back to order. Then, police boy lost it. He charged into the group, rolled up newspaper in hand, and swatted at kids. They fought back. They knocked over desks, kids fell down. Erika yelled, girls screamed, boys swung at each other.

It took about ten minutes, but Mrs. Gordon did a good job of shouting the whole group back into submission and putting the furniture in the room back together. She asked me to debrief the experiment. I felt stunned, like when you try a magic trick and it works. I asked the observers to speak. Their insights were great—how the environment creates problems, how close to the surface some hidden feelings are, and how some people shouldn't be police officers.

Still, I guessed I might get an F in psych for causing a riot, and I wondered whether Sister Agnes would be waiting outside the classroom because of the noise, or if Mrs. Gordon would report me after class was over. By the time I got to my next class, rumors of the riot had spread, and I slithered through the hallways, hoping to avoid Sister Agnes. Strike three, I imagined her saying.

It didn't matter anyway. This would be my last time in school.

My plan after high school was to take the full-time job offered by the restaurant where I worked. My friend Betsy from Sarvis Park had gotten me the job. In my deepest fantasies, I wanted to marry David. Though I got decent grades in the highest-level classes and always scored well on standardized tests, I hadn't thought about college. When they called an assembly for kids planning for college, I didn't attend, and didn't set up an appointment with a counselor to discuss it.

My Sarvis park friends weren't going to college. Some in the Sarvis bike gang had graduated to real gangs, from bikes to motorcycles, from drinking to drugs, from shoplifting to B&Es. Some girls had gotten pregnant. The boys were mostly getting ready for Vietnam. I didn't have much time to hang out with them, though. I was busy at school during the day, working at night, and watching my younger brother on weekends. Having money in my pockets gave me freedom.

It was Tuesday and that night I called David. He told me that when he was called up he planned to be a conscientious objector. I told him I couldn't make it on Friday and let him know I had date with someone else. I wouldn't lie to him. I could tell by the slam on the other end of the line he wasn't happy to hear it and probably wouldn't forgive me.

On Wednesday night, Trudy dropped by my house. She wanted to know whether I was going to a concert up north on Friday. As she talked, she twisted a gold ring on the index finger of her left hand several times.

"Are you going steady with someone?" I asked, actually happy for her because she always seemed to just miss in relationships.

"James gave it to me. He's going to Vietnam and we decided to step it up before he left."

This surprised me. I was a little hurt, but maybe a little relieved. I thought James and I were going together, but apparently, he had another thing going with someone else at the same time. For years, Trudy had been trying to get James's attention, but he'd ignored her.

She smiled.

We'd always had a weird relationship. She had liked James, and he liked me. She liked David, and he asked me out. She seemed to pit herself against me, or at least imagined I was in competition with her. She was the person who'd called me a spic and spread lies about me stealing pens in middle school. During late middle school, she started hanging out with the same Sarvis Park kids I did, though.

I would not get in her way. If she and James liked each other, that was enough for me to step aside. Later that night I called James and told him I didn't want to go out on Friday. I was an ice princess.

It wasn't until years later, after we talked when he came back from Vietnam, that I learned Trudy made the whole thing up, ring and all, and had never even spoken to him.

On Friday, since neither David nor James now wanted to go out with me, I called friends to go to the concert. I worked. I owned a car. My friends expected me to drive. They each chipped in a dollar for gas and crammed into my green Dodge with its push button transmission and bald tires.

We were hurrying back because the concert, about two hours north of Flint, lasted past their curfews. *Question Mark and the Mysterians* played nothing but variations on *96 Tears* over and over, but we stayed until the very end. As we raced home it began to rain, then the temperature dropped. The rain turned the ground slick and a mist covered the road.

I didn't see the curve until I was in it, heading straight at almost seventy miles per hour, while the road turned sharply to the left. When I hit the brakes and jerked the steering wheel, the car began to spin. I somehow remembered to *pump the breaks and steer into the curve*, the words written in my driver's training manual, but the car ignored me and continued to spin.

We began to donut across two lanes of highway.

A huge oak tree stood on the other side of the road directly in our path. I knew we would hit it at an awful speed, and there was nothing I could do. The car wasn't responding.

My body wanted to brace for the impact, but instead it got weird. It slowed down. Just like the cliché. As though I were watching a home movie, I saw my life. First, images from infancy. It felt like I was recalling them for the first time, but I recognized them. Next, my early childhood played out in front of me. Then, scenes from my later childhood and early teens. I saw conversations that had taken place, events, scenes, people. Everything, seemingly every moment, came back to me in order. As each scenario unfolded, it was as though a question was being posed to me: Had I done the right thing? Had I said the right thing? Had I been helpful?

I swear I never had a second thought about most events, but on that night, spinning across the highway, I realized I had hurt people. I had often done the most selfish thing.

As my memories caught up to the present, I saw the huge oak tree coming straight at me, getting larger and larger in the windshield.

I will never forget when my front bumper made contact with that tree.

When I composed myself enough to step out of the car and look, it appeared the front bumper kissed the tree. No crash, no damage, just a soft stop, the car gently touching the base of the big oak.

Everyone else was already out of the car hugging each other. They pounded my back, congratulating me for being a great driver. I'd done nothing other than endangering them in the first place.

When we drove away, I thought, not about the almost-crash, or even the whole-life-review-time-slowing-down thing, but about the questions that came with it. It was as though I was being reminded that what I did in life mattered to other people, not just me.

I was almost at the end of my school year. I'd received an invitation to Senior Honors Night. When I looked around the room decorated with fancy tables and flowers, I was embarrassed to see I was the only person without a parent. Most kids even had two. I didn't know why I'd been invited.

As awards were handed out, *First Honors, Second Honors, Honorable Mention,* the name of the planned university of attendance followed each award. Sister Agnes called my name.

"Honorable Mention, Art and Psychology," she said, adding a long pause, making it obvious no college was in my future.

When I sat down, I saw both my awards were for *First Honors,* the top awards possible, not *Honorable Mention* as she said. I wondered whether she made a mistake or decided I shouldn't be publicly acknowledged—a last jab at me. *Strike three?* I wondered about the difference between one teacher who wanted to reward me and one who wanted to punish me.

The next week I stopped by Mrs. Gordon's classroom to thank her for nominating me for the award. As I clapped erasers together, she asked me where I was going to college. I explained, no, I wasn't going to college, they'd offered me a full-time job as a waitress at Wally's Supper Club.

"Oh. I just assumed you would go to college," she said. The look on her face surprised me—disappointment. My mother seemed pleased I wasn't going to college; it would save her an expense and I could help with my brother. I was lucky to have a full-time job already with my friend Betsy working at the same place. But someone, one adult I respected who also respected me, even though I'd caused a riot in her classroom, thought I was capable.

Over that summer I watched the other waitresses, most of them much older than me. They were kind and treated me generously, even though I was a self-centered little twit, never making their lives easier by helping out with extras.

One very busy day at the restaurant, a man stood up and blocked my path as I carried a full tray of food. He was angry because he'd asked me for mustard for his sandwich *three times*, he yelled. As I got his mustard, it occurred to me I was not a good waitress. I didn't care if people got food. The other waitresses seemed to enjoy the job, but I felt like my air supply was closing off. I was just going through the motions.

Later that night, when I walked out to the nearly empty parking lot, I heard shuffling behind me. When I turned, the man whose mustard I'd forgotten was on me before I could register what he was doing. He pushed his arm under my chin and pinned me against the building. I tried to move my arms, but he pressed his chest against me. He used his free hand to reach under the white skirt of my uniform, grabbed the top of my panty hose and panties, yanking down on them hard.

I couldn't breathe.

His face was close to mine and I could see the look in his eyes, his arm almost lifting me off the ground. Before he could yank my clothes any further, something smashed against the side of his head, knocking him off of me.

Betsy's purse, with its gold metallic frame, was raised to strike again as she yelled, *"Get the fuck away."*

A small group of busboys walking out to the parking lot stepped into view then came toward us. The man ran for his car and jumped in. His tires squealed when he peeled out of the parking lot, while I bent over trying to catch my breath. Everyone grouped around me, cussing the asshole out. They walked me to my car. I thanked Betsy many times because she'd likely saved my life.

The next day, before our shifts started, Betsy and I sat at a corner booth near the kitchen reserved for waitresses and retold the story to the other women, discussing what could have happened if I had been alone.

"Weren't you scared?" someone asked.

"I didn't have time to think about it."

What I remembered was the look in his eyes.

I recognized that look. It was the same look Trudy had when she called me a spic. It was the same look Sister Agnes sometimes gave me when she watched me. *Who do you think you are? Do you think you are as good as me? I can prove you're not by doing something to you.* Behind that look something else was there, some kind of fear, something needing to strike out. *If I'm not better than you then what am I?*

"Shit, this is the second thing that happened to me recently, and I didn't feel fear when I should have." I told them about the spin out in my car, how we all walked away, how it made me wonder what I was doing with my life.

"What *are* you doing here?" Betsy asked.

"What are *you* doing here?" I responded, with my usual snappy comeback. *I'd be lucky to be like you, since I'm always taken by surprise. You aren't.*

"I like this job. This is fun for me. It's not fun for you. Everyone can tell," she said. I looked around the table. They all agreed, I could tell. I didn't like being a waitress, but I was so afraid of losing these waitresses as friends. I finally understood.

I hadn't recognized I felt fear because I was already afraid.

Since I'd moved to Flint in fifth grade, I'd developed a low-grade fear, like a temperature just below the fever point. Fear of being isolated, of being left out. Of losing the people around me—my father dying, my mother being sick, my friends disappearing. Of losing friends like these waitresses, who would protect me, even if I didn't deserve it. Words from *Dune,* the book in my purse, came to mind: "Fear is the mind killer."

The questions from my spin-out flash came to me. Was I saying the right thing?

"Thank you for being there last night. And thanks for pointing out it out, I know I'm not cut out for this job."

If I didn't want to be a waitress, what did I want? I wasn't a child anymore, but I still wanted the chance to go out and see the world, to explore as I had when I was ten—without fear. It was time to do what I wanted and needed to do. To do what was right. It was time for me to fight.

That summer I waited tables and earned enough money to pay my way for a first semester at the local community college.

EPILOGUE

Eventually, I transferred to the state university. For an undergraduate major I chose languages—Spanish, the language I'd all but forgotten, and Chinese because I wanted a challenge. I remembered that the time in my life when I felt happiest, I was speaking multiple languages.

The things I thought worked against me now strangely worked in my favor. Coming from a multi-ethnic background helped me feel comfortable at a large university with an international community. My exposure to languages when I was young—Spanish, Greek, Latin, Arabic—all helped with standardized tests and science classes. My love of reading gave me an advantage with my assignments. Having gone to small Catholic schools where I took advanced classes prepared me for college coursework. My friends from Sarvis Park prepped me for living in a student ghetto with people from different backgrounds. Because I had already been exposed to drinking and drugging, I didn't get pulled in those directions. I saw many friends get pulled off track with those things when they first experienced the freedom of college.

The things I thought others disliked about me actually prepared me.

Later, when I received a Ph.D., I made toasts to Mrs. Gordon, the educator who had the most impact on my life, to Betsy, who saved my life in more ways than one, and to Isaac Asimov because *Foundation* inspired my dissertation.

My friend James eventually married his real high school sweetheart. My friend David moved to the country and opened a Buddhist retreat center. I remembered that once Trudy showed up at Sarvis park with a large handprint on her face, so I knew she came from a tough place, and I decided the best way to deal with her was to forgive her. We became good friends. I was a bridesmaid at her wedding. I became friends with most of the people from my high school.

233

I married an attorney, with his two kids. With three additions, I finally got to create the warm, caring family I always wanted, though the marriage didn't survive.

We still hold reunions of the Sarvis Park bike gang, at least those of us who survived to adulthood.

The things that *might* have destroyed me—going from being a Puerto Rican princess to being called a spic, to being called an immigrant, and to being a hood rat—made me stronger. Being attacked in a parking lot and spinning out in my car lit a fire for me. I had to fight for myself and for what I wanted to happen in my life. To do the right things. To rewrite the scripts handed to me.

Many of my middle school and high school years in Flint were spent underwater, not fitting in, struggling to find friends, struggling with loss and grief and loneliness. A few people stood up for me. I got tougher. Had I remained a princess, I probably wouldn't have done so.

At one time in my life I believed I could breathe under water. At one time I was pushed and held down below the surface. The ocean can be dangerous. It raises you up, carries you out and takes you places you didn't plan to go. I still sometimes dream about a woman stepping out of the ocean. I had to own that I was part of the ocean, not separate from it, and I have no control over it, only how I react to it.

You have to find strength wherever you are, ocean or desert. It's important to figure out when to breathe and when not to breathe underwater.

ACKNOWLEDGMENTS AND GRATITUDES

I have to start by giving thanks to my wonderful, diverse family. As Italian, Puerto Rican, Syrian, Jordanian, Mexican, Irish, English, Danish, Chinese, etc. etc. they know how to create happiness and love in many cultures. A boost of love goes forward to my grandchildren. Their presence in my life brings endless joy.

The story was told because my father, Angelo Juan Morciglio, a decorated World War II veteran from Yauco, Puerto Rico, and my mother, Lottie Shaheen, a fashion designer from Flint, Michigan, of Syrian descent, had the courage to fight the racial prejudices of their times, and elope. Their bravery continues to inspire me.

Other groups of people in this story deserve acknowledgment and thanks: my friends from the "Sarvis Park bike gang" in Flint, Michigan, Judy, Mary, Susie, Sue, Jeff, Lonny, Bobby, Pat and the many others, who rode their bikes and saved me at the time of my life I needed saving most. Thanks to my Syrian relatives and cousins whom I now love and adore.

I'd also like to acknowledge people I never thought about thanking when growing up but had so much influence on my life: my teachers. Particularly Mrs. Love-appropriately named, Mr. Paul Rozycki, and Mrs. Barbara Gordon, my Psychology teacher who convinced me to go to college with one look.. So many of my teachers were good role models, but I didn't figure that out until much later in life.

A special thanks goes to the Bloomingdale Writers Connection and the Friends of the Bloomingdale Regional Library, for their support of Life Story Writing program. Val Perry, our fearless leader, is a continuous source of inspiration. Her dedication to this program has sent hundreds of people on a journey of lifelong reflection and created dozens of writing groups.

A thank you goes to the people in my writers' groups, Saturday Write Live, and the Sun City Writers, and to Mike Birch, for the patience to read this work in the raw.

Finally, thanks to my co-conspirators on this book, who graciously came along for the ride, opening my eyes to many dimensions of identity.

Figure 8 -John (Angelo Juan) Morciglio, circa 1944.

Figure 9 – Lottie (Latifay) Shaheen, circa 1944.

Figure 10 -The wedding of John and Lottie Morciglio, 1945.

Figure 11 – The Morciglio family on the steps of their hotel, 1962, the beginning of Jean's story. John, Jean, Chris, Lottie, and Johnny.

ABOUT THE AUTHORS

Betty Viamontes, CPA, MBA

Betty Viamontes is the author of four novels and an anthology of short stories. Her novel, *Waiting on Zapote Street,* is a winner of the *Latino Books Into Movies* Award. The Latino Author website lists this autobiographical novel as one of the best ten books of 2016. In 2017, it became an Amazon bestseller, after being selected by a United Nations women's book club and multiple others. *"The Girl from White Creek,"* her latest book, was Amazon's #1 new release. Her works have appeared in various publications, including the University of South Florida's literary journal *The Mailer Review.* She holds two master's degrees from the University of South Florida, as well as a Graduate Certificate in Creative Writing.

https://twitter.com/bviamont
https://www.facebook.com/betty.viamontes
https://www.linkedin.com/in/betty-viamontes-cpa-mba-69674466/
https://www.instagram.com/bettyviamontes/

Anna Brubaker, M.Ed.

Anna Brubaker is originally from the U.S. state of Indiana, but has lived in Ohio and, now, in Florida for the past 27 years. Trained as a journalist, her published writing career began when she won Seventeen Magazine's annual Short Story Contest as a teenager. She has since written newspaper articles, advertisements, short stories, plays, dramatic monologues, and educational materials. She is currently working on her first fiction novel. She has taught Life Story Writing as part of the Bloomingdale Writers Connection Life Story Writing program in Valrico, Florida. A married mother and grandmother, Anna is a public school special education teacher who enjoys cross-stitch, cooking, baseball, and visiting museums and historical sites. Anna strives for authenticity and raw truth in her writing, and honors all who are brave enough to tell their own stories to the world.

https://www.facebook.com/Aquamarine-Media-2070796779810319

Susana Jiménez-Mueller, MSBC

Susana, a Cuban-American writer, is the author of *Now I Swim,* and collaborator of *Perico - The Amazing Burro.* She writes prose and poetry about love for family, genealogy, and the microscopic. Susana holds a Master in Business Continuity Management from Norwich University, a Bachelor in Chemistry from Florida International University, and a writing certificate from the Institute of Children's Literature. She teaches Life Story Writing and leads the Bloomingdale Regional Library *Life Stories Enrich (LISTEN) Project,* producing audio recordings for writers in Valrico, Florida. Susana is an avid genealogist and family storyteller. She is presently working on a novel based on her family, dating to colonial times in Cuba.

www.susanasbooks.com
susana@susanas-books.com
https://twitter.com/susanas_books
www.facebook/susanasbooks
Linkedin.com/in/susanamueller
https://www.instagram.com/susanasbooks/

Jean F. Morciglio, PhD

Jean Morciglio is an author and instructor with over 35 years working in higher education. She has experience writing and publishing literary essays, short stories, and research papers for industry journals and colleges, most recently publishing creative non-fiction in the *Story Circle Network* and the *Florida Odet Literary Journal.* Her book, *What high school students really think about community colleges*, focuses on decoding public opinion and addresses the stigma of community colleges. A certified autobiographer, Jean helps writers craft their own stories of their past and present selves, teaching guided life story writing in Valrico, Florida. She has a passion for providing learners with the tools to define their own narrative and discover who they are in the process.

Jean@Jeanmorciglio.com
flowing.glass.publications@gmail.com
www.jeanmorciglio.com
@jeanmorciglio
https://www.linkedin.com/in/jeanmorciglio/
www.jmorciglio.com.

BOOK CLUB DISCUSSION QUESTIONS

Like Finding Water in the Desert is a memoir anthology written by four women with Hispanic roots. The book is divided into four themed sections: Reclaiming, Redefining, Reconciling, and Rewriting. The following questions compiled from various book-club websites (see links below) can be used to discuss the stories separately or the anthology in its entirety.

1. "What was your initial reaction to the book? Did it hook you immediately, or take some time to get into?
2. Each woman speaks to a different theme. How do the themes of their stories differ?
    - Did you feel like you got the 'true' story?
    - Did they start too slow or end unresolved?
    - Do you wish they had been told from a different perspective?
    - Did they jump around too much or hold you in suspense?
3. What tests did each woman face?
    - Did you approve of their decisions and behavior?
    - Who did you relate to the most/least?
    - Are there any quotes, passages, or scenes you found particularly compelling?
    - Were there parts of the book you thought were incredibly unique, out of place, thought-provoking, or disturbing?
4. How does the theme of "finding water in the desert" surface in each story?
    - What were the main points you think the authors were trying to make?
    - Did you notice any symbolism?

5. What did you think about the ending?
   - Were you satisfied or disappointed with how the stories ended?
   - Is anything left unresolved or ambiguous?
   - How do you picture the characters' lives after the end of the story?
6. Each woman has Hispanic roots, but is exposed to different cultures. How do their cultures differ?
7. What changes/decisions would you hope for if the book were turned into a movie?
   - Which sections would you cut?
   - Who would you cast to play the main characters?
   - If the book is already a movie, are you happy with the representation? Do you prefer the book or the movie?
8. How does this book compare to other books you've read?
   - Did you like it more or less than other books in the same genre?
   - Is the book different in any way from the books you usually read?
9. How did this book change you?
   - Do you feel different now than you did before you read it?
   - Do you have a new perspective as a result of reading this book?
   - Did you learn something you didn't know before?
   - Has your attitude or behavior changed?"

https://www.book-club-guide.com/book-club-discussion-questions.html

https://www.bustle.com/articles/167822-13-general-book-club-questions-for-any-kind-of-discussion
https://wondermomwannabe.com/book-club-questions/

WITHDRAWN

CPSIA information can be obtained
at www.ICGtesting.com
Printed in the USA
LVHW040512230921
698482LV00001B/155

9 781734 137736